CAREER MISCONDUCT

THE STORY OF BILL WIRTZ'S GREED, CORRUPTION, AND THE BETRAYAL OF BLACKHAWKS' FANS

MARK WEINBERG

Blueline Publishing, Inc.
Chicago

ISBN 0-9656312-0-6

Printed in the United States.
First Edition.

Cataloging in publication data is on file at the Library of
Congress and is available from Blueline Publishing, Inc.

Blueline Publishing, Inc.
3612 N. Tripp Ave. Chicago, IL 60641
Ph: 773.283.3913
e-mail: blueline@mcs.com.

Career Misconduct can purchased at
www.careermisconduct.com. Special discounted rates
available for bulk orders. Call the publisher.

Editors' note: No names in this book have been
changed to protect the guilty.

In memory of LKW
1927 — 1997

Acknowledgements

I am grateful to my family and friends who helped me with this book. Some of my friends read the manuscript and told me it was outstanding, which, believe me, I know means nothing, since lying is part of the job requirement. But I greatly appreciated the encouragement. Some friends listened patiently to me as I talked about the book for over a year and a half, and they too lied, telling me that it all sounded very interesting and that they couldn't wait to read it. And then there were my best friends and closest family members who neither read the manuscript, nor encouraged me to write the book, nor were even much interested in talking to me about it, but simply wanted me to finish "the gaddamn thing already." I'm thankful to all for different reasons. They are: Jane Alexander, David Cromwell, Winston Drake, Todd Feldman, Becca Feldman, Jackie Feldman, Mark Finch, Miriam Fisch, Matthew Flegenheimer, Mark Frohlich, Martha Furst, Susie Furst, John Gerber, Donald Gries, Lynn-Anne Gries, Jim Griffin, Julie Hauselman, Hillary Jay, Ben Joravski, Rachel Kaplan, Rachel Klugman, Lisa Stein Kornfeld, Bernard Kramer, Julia Kramer, Perri Kramer, Chad Larson, Nancy Kohn, Steve Kohn, Caroline Loeb, Doug Masters, Marty Oberman, Scott Reicin, Frank Rice, Annie Rosenthal, Pat Shannon, Jim Siergey, Greg Simetz, Steve Stern, Elaine Weinberg, Jill Weinberg, Peter Weinberg, and Sidney Weinberg. Special thanks to George Hradecky for helping with the drafting of chapter Seven and his close line-reading of the finished manuscript; to Sucheep "Aek" Sukkajonwong for his cover design; and to Mike Gallagher for being my computer 'genius' friend over the last 10 years — he designs an awesome website (see www.careermisconduct.com). Thanks, too, to all the readers of *The Blue Line* who supported us over the eight years we published the program from 1991-1997. Now, I hope you buy the book.

Contents

Introduction

"It is a sin to believe evil of others,
but it is seldom a mistake."

— *H. L. Mencken*

In Chicago, Bill Wirtz is best known as the owner of the Chicago Blackhawks, but beyond that he is also one of the richest men in the world. In its October 2000 issue, *Forbes* magazine, our society's chronicler of the wealthy elite, estimated that there were 298 billionaires in America and 482 billionaires across the globe, and Bill Wirtz is certainly one of them.[1] The Wirtz family guards its financial data zealously, but what is known is this: Wirtz's major assets include the Chicago Blackhawks, the United Center, several liquor distributors, exclusive real estate, banking interests, and substantial stock holdings. The Blackhawks themselves are valued at close to $200 million. The United Center, of which Wirtz owns 50 percent, is worth at least $200 million. *Crain's Chicago Business* estimates that Wirtz also owns approximately 100 residential buildings, most of them near or on the Chicago lakefront, and owns one of Chicago's premier commercial properties, the 333 N. Michigan Ave. office building. An average property on

---

[1]"The 400 Richest People In America," October 9, 2000 *Forbes,* p. 117. Wirtz was not included on *Forbes'* list of the richest Americans, but that is certainly not because he isn't one. It's because his company is not public — indeed, in general his family has very few public holdings — and Wirtz is notorious for the secrecy of his business operations. As a result, his wealth cannot be easily evaluated, unlike the growing number of internet paper billionaires. Moreover, much of Wirtz's assets are held in family trusts, and *Forbes* looks at combined family assets differently than it does individual holdings.

Chicago's lakefront is conservatively worth $20 million, which puts Wirtz's real estate holding alone at $2 billion.[2]

Wirtz is also the eighth-largest beverage distributor in the U.S., owning a collection of liquor distributors in various states, including Judge & Dolph Ltd., which sells approximately 33% of all wine and liquor in Illinois. Other Wirtz-owned distributorships exist in Wisconsin, Texas, Nevada and Minnesota. According to court filings in 1999, Wirtz's liquor distributorships have annual sales of approximately $750 million.[3] In addition, public records reveal that Wirtz owns 6,451,122 shares of Firstar Bank, a multi-state bank holding company that owns over 1,200 banks in 12 states. The stock currently has a market value of more than $148 million. In addition, Wirtz owns 1,754,000 shares of Alberto-Culver Co. with a current market value of over $52 million. (Since he sits on the board of directors of both these companies, these two stocks are the only ones that Wirtz is compelled to disclose by law.) He also owns numerous parking lots, as well as horse farms in Illinois and Ohio, and several independent banks, including 100% of First Security Trust & Savings Bank in Elmwood Park, Illinois, and 72% of First National Bank of South Miami, Florida. All told, even a conservative estimate of Wirtz's assets brings them to between $3 — $4 billion.

But Wirtz's incredible wealth and status is only part of the story. The purpose of this book is to document Bill Wirtz's repeated acts of corruption, criminality, and lies. Taken as a whole, the book reveals an undeniable and startling pattern of corruption and lawlessness, including repeated violations of the antitrust laws, bribery, political payoffs, perjury, theft, collusion against NHL players, and monumental greed. For many readers, the exposure of Wirtz's criminality will not be a big surprise. Few businessmen anywhere have as bad a public reputation as Bill Wirtz, and thus much of what I reveal in this book will only serve to confirm what many already suspect about the man. But even if I am preaching to the converted, I hope the specific details of lawbreaking and corruption will serve to solidify the suspicions that already exist about Wirtz. It's enough if this book simply confirms that what people "know" about Wirtz is, in fact, true.

At the outset, it must be said that this book is not the story of a man's life. I don't presume to know all there is to know about Bill Wirtz. I am sure he has many wonderful qualities, none of which I discuss here. This book is all Hyde, no Jekyll. A critic in the *New York Times* recently wrote, "What's good

[2]Jeff Borden "Banks, Booze, Buildings, Blackhawks, Too: Inside The World Of Bill Wirtz," *Crain's Chicago Business*, April 14, 1997, p. 1.

[3]Joseph T. Hallihan and Douglas Holt, "How The Wirtzes Sold Liquor Law," *Chicago Tribune*, Nov. 12, 1999, p. 1N.

about a well-done polemic is that everything fits neatly into place. What's bad about a well-done polemic is that everything fits neatly into place."[4] I believe there is enormous value in showing that the Emperor has no clothes, but it is myopic and wrongheaded to see Bill Wirtz as a cartoon-like character of pure evil. Proper perspective demands acknowledging that not every act undertaken by him is corrupt and base, but proper perspective also demands acknowledging that he's engaged in a sustained pattern and practice of corrupt behavior throughout his professional life.

Why write such a book? Exposing various instances of Wirtz's illegalities and corruption is not the untold story of the Bay of Pigs, but how the wealthiest and most powerful members of our society use their power is not a trivial matter either. It is incredibly dangerous for corrupt behavior of any sort to go unpunished and unexposed. Doing so leads to ever greater corruption, for when corrupt behavior goes unpunished it rewards those who engage in corruption, associating corruption with achievement. And it is especially dangerous for corrupt behavior by our society's most privileged to go unexposed and uncondemned, for when society's privileged get away with flouting the law, it undermines the very notion of law-abidingness.

I know many people will dub this book negative, spiteful, hurtful and malicious. But, practically speaking, the public exposure and condemnation of Wirtz's skulduggery is the only check on the abuse of his private economic power. It is nearly impossible to take away a billionaire's financial capital, but the one thing that can be taken away is his reputational capital. In our society, billionaires are well insulated from almost all traditional forms of justice: there's no confronting them directly, no throwing them out of office, no possibility of public protest to alter their behavior, and no countervailing political or monetary power to control their actions. Moreover, the courts are a slow and uncertain vehicle for obtaining justice and are really every billionaire's preferred forum, since his resources allow him to drag out legal proceedings for decades and money damages are the only punishment that a civil court can ultimately impose, which is no real threat to a billionaire's well-being. And on top of everything else, certain indecencies committed by those with enormous economic clout simply can't be reduced to narrow, legal questions.

It seems to me especially important to condemn the crimes of the wealthy today. We live in money-mad society where making money is viewed as a sign of intelligence and wherewithal no matter how it is achieved. There seems to be a monstrous sense of forgiveness towards the crimes of the wealthy, along with an insufficient desire by most people to dis-

[4]Karen Lehrman, "10,000 Things I Hate About You," *New York Times*, May 9, 1999, Book Review section, p. 12.

tinguish between making money in an honorable and respectable way from making it in a dishonorable way. In exposing Bill Wirtz's pattern of abuses, I hope to suggest that, rich and powerful though he may be, he is undeserving of our society's respect. I hope to echo the words of the great muckraking journalist Ida Tarbell, who exposed the depredations of John D. Rockefeller in the early 1900s. In her autobiography, *All In A Day's Work*, she wrote of Rockefeller and his cohorts at Standard Oil: "They had never played fair, and that ruined their greatness for me."[5]

In writing this book, I also hope to counter the misrepresentations and lies offered by the Blackhawks' PR people about Wirtz. In all their public relations efforts, the Blackhawks present Bill Wirtz as a model citizen, a philanthropist, a man deserving of the community's highest admiration and respect. They call Bill Wirtz "a great man," "a man of great character," and "a model humanitarian," and they insist that if people knew him better, they would like him more.[6] Without even winking or crossing his fingers, Bob Pulford routinely praises Wirtz for his impeccable integrity:

> People don't know Bill Wirtz. They think he's worried about money all the time and call him 'Dollar Bill.' That's the exact opposite of the man. It's unjustified. It bothers me to hear people say things about him. He is an extremely honest and moral person. To a fault, almost. He won't do anything under the table. Everything has to be straight. Let's put it this way: If he was coaching in the NCAA, he'd never be in violation of the rules.[7]

And Elvis lives.

PR is PR of course, and the Blackhawks have every right to spread the manure any way they see fit, even if it means ignoring reality. At the same time, though, others have the right to dig beneath the surface of the standard PR hype and alter the air-brushed portrait that the Blackhawks present of

---

[5]Ron Chernow, *Titan: The Life of John D. Rockefeller, Sr.*, Random House, New York, 1998, p. 433.

[6]Concerning his boss' negative public reputation, Blackhawks' director of public relations, Jim DeMaria, has insisted, "People who get to know him [Bill Wirtz] change their opinion of him." See *Weinberg and Blue Line Publishing, Inc. v. Chicago Blackhawks Hockey Team*, Case No. 96-L1099, Circuit Court of Cook County, County Department, Law Division. Jim DeMaria, Tr. 363-364, 24:1.

[7]Mike Kiley, "NHL owners love Wirtz — Even If Hawks Fans Don't," *Chicago Tribune*, January 18, 1991, p. 3C. Pulford's fervid defense of Wirtz bring to mind the philosopher Reinhold Neibuhr's notion of "frantic orthodoxy." "Frantic orthodoxy," Niebuhr wrote, "is never rooted in faith but in doubt. It is when we are not sure that we are doubly sure."

Wirtz. It is my hope that the force and specificity of the facts of corruption and illegality detailed here will make it clear that Wirtz's public reputation is not the result of any "misunderstanding" but that, if anything, Bill Wirtz is understood all too well by the public.

The emphasis of this book is on *provable* facts. This book is not an Oliver Stone movie that takes factual liberties to make a point. I do not want anyone to be able to dismiss this book as mere rhetoric, and any unsupported claims or exaggerations by me would undoubtedly be pounced upon by Wirtz's PR apparatus to diminish this book's credibility. To support my charges against Wirtz, I felt it incumbent upon me to provide readers with detailed footnotes so that all my charges can be confirmed by anyone interested in doing so. I have also scrupulously cited court records to provide readers with the means to substantiate all legal claims made against Wirtz. And besides, the taking of factual liberties wasn't necessary here, as Bill Wirtz has done enough provable criminal behavior that one doesn't have to make up anything in order to present him as a rather remarkable example of dishonesty and corruption.[8]

These days everybody attacks everybody for being a "law-breaking, greedy corporate bastard." Environmentalists, the human rights activists, the consumer activists — they all throw epithets around with reckless glee. In most cases, the condemnation is unsupported by the hard-to-uncover facts and can thus be easily dismissed. But a full, accurate reporting of the facts of Wirtz's corruption can't be so easily dismissed. In presenting the evidence assembled here, my goal was to make the case against Wirtz so tight and sound, both legally and factually, that in case he — or, more accurately, his armada of lawyers — wanted to sue anybody for matters disclosed in this book, they would have only one person to sue — Bill Wirtz himself for defamation of his own character.

In the interest of full disclosure, I must say that I am not simply writing this book as an academic exercise. I have had my own run-ins with Bill Wirtz and have seen first-hand the kind of ruthless business tactics he uses against his business competitors. For eight years, from February of 1991 thru December of 1997, I published an unofficial hockey program, called *The Blue Line*. *The Blue Line* was sold outside of every Chicago Blackhawks home game and competed with the Blackhawks' own hockey program, called

---

[8]The crimes and corruption revealed here are almost surely just the tip of the iceberg. The whole story can't be written because most of the stories are well hidden. Pay-offs, bribery, collusion — these things aren't exactly shouted from the mountaintop. Like other powerful, corrupt figures, Bill Wirtz prefers to bask in the shadows of his power, having others do his bidding while he plays the master puppeteer, using his underlings to protect him from any taint of suspicion.

Face Off. The Blue Line was cheaper, funnier, naughtier and more objective than the Blackhawks' program, and it quickly became the unofficial program of Blackhawks' fans. *The Blue Line* was also highly critical of the Blackhawks' team and engaged in harsh satirical criticism of Blackhawks' management, including Bill Wirtz.

In response, the Blackhawks did everything they could to hurt *The Blue Line*'s business, including calling up advertisers to have them pull their ads. For instance, insiders at Coors Beer have told us that Bill Wirtz himself called the headquarters of Coors Beer in Golden, Colorado and told them, "It wasn't in their best interests to continue advertising in *The Blue Line*." Under oath, Bill Wirtz has denied making such a call, but soon after Wirtz allegedly made it, Coors Beer pulled its advertisements from *The Blue Line*. The company gave us no reason for pulling its ad and refused to even take back any of the money it had pre-paid for its advertising. We later learned that Bill Wirtz owns several Coors distributors in several states.

The Blackhawks also refused to grant *The Blue Line* media credentials. The denial of media credentials prevented T*he Blue Line* from gaining access to the pressbox and attending post-game interviews, press conferences, and practices, and it was a severe blow to *The Blue Line*'s ability to cover the team and enhance its own editorial content. The denial of media credentials virtually eliminated *The Blue Line*'s ability to provide its readers with player and coaches' interviews and feature stories, thus marginalizing *The Blue Line* and giving the Blackhawks' program, *Face Off*, a competitive advantage.

In response, I sued the Blackhawks in 1992 under the Illinois Antitrust law, claiming that the Blackhawks' tactics were a classic form of monopoly leveraging, whereby a monopolist uses its power in one market to create a competitive advantage for itself in another. In a nutshell, the Blackhawks were using their control of the live presentation of NHL hockey and their control over press credentials to create an unfair advantage for themselves in the market for game-day hockey programs.

I brought the case filled with Erin Brockovich-visions dancing in my head, knowing the law and the facts were on my side. But suing the Blackhawks and Bill Wirtz turned out to be a nightmare. The Blackhawks' lawyers used every trick in the legal handbook to draw the case out for over nine years, including delay tactics, obfuscation, obstruction of justice, and blatant lying. They challenged every argument, "accidentally" threw out important evidence, fought over the discovery of every piece of evidence and exhausted me with paper work. The poet Stevie Smith has written: "It is the privilege of the rich to waste the time of the poor." No truer statement about litigation (at least versus a billionaire) has ever been written. Over the course of nine years of battling the Hawks in court, I spent tens of thousands of dollars and wasted thousands of hours (I was my own lawyer, and as the old saying goes, a lawyer who represents himself has a fool for a client). In the end, it was all to no avail. In June 2000, after the case had gone up to the Illinois Supreme Court and back down to the trial court, the case was dismissed by the trial judge in favor of the Blackhawks before it got to trial. The judge ruled that the two programs —*The Blue Line* and *Face Off*— were *not* in competition with each other, thus undermining the whole premise on which the lawsuit was based.[9]

By writing this little handbook of Wirtz's corruptions, I feel I have answered a challenge imposed on me by the Blackhawks themselves. The Blackhawks repeatedly denounced the satire in *The Blue Line* directed at Bill Wirtz as "unfair" and "defamatory." They claimed that the reason they denied *The Blue Line* media credentials was that it "grossly misrepresented" everything Bill Wirtz stood for. But by substantiating with indisputable factual evidence the illicit, untoward business activities that the satire in *The Blue Line* played off of and mocked, I hope this book serves as a counterpunch to the Blackhawks' charges.

Some readers may find the earnest reporting of Wirtz's crimes and the biting satirical commentary in *The Blue Line* at odds with one another, but they are just two alternate forms of social criticism — one diminishing through ridicule, the other through evidence and rational argument. In chapter Nine, I have included several examples of the "crude," "sordid," "salacious," "obscene" satire found in *The Blue Line*. In addition, throughout the book, I have used original cartoons and mock photographs intended to skewer Wirtz and his business methods. And for those readers who do find the mixture of serious factual reporting and prickly humor to be jarring, I quote the poet Robert Frost who said in a letter to a friend, "You might think I am joking, but I am never so serious as when I am."

And now let the crimes begin.

---

[9]It was an incredibly bad ruling, contrary to all the evidence, and anyone who wants to go out for a beer and listen to me cry about it can call me. I'm buying. I know complaining about a legal ruling makes one sound like big crybaby, but — damn it— it was bad, bad, bad! Why doesn't anybody believe me? Technically speaking, the case isn't over. It is currently on appeal to the Illinois Appellate Court, but the odds of overturning the lower court are about the same as a Blackhawks winning the Stanley Cup. See *Weinberg and Blue Line Publishing, Inc. v. Chicago Blackhawks Hockey Team*, Case No. 96-L1099, Circuit Court of Cook County, County Department, Law Division.

"Listen, son, I've decided to establish a legal defense fund for you while you're still young and unindicted."

CHAPTER 1

The Illegal Monopolization
of Professional Boxing in the 1950s

*"Nobody talks more of free enterprise and competition
and of the best man winning than the man
who inherited his father's store."*

— *C. Wright Mills*

In 1957, Bill Wirtz's father, Arthur Wirtz, and Arthur's partner, Jim Norris, Jr., were found guilty of illegally monopolizing the promotion and exhibition of professional championship boxing in the United States. The case involves blackmail, extortion, phony bookkeeping, bribery, and mob violence. At the time this case was first filed by the U.S. government in March of 1952, Bill Wirtz would have been just 21 years old, and there is no reason to think he was involved in the family's illegal practices. But it is important to begin our story with Arthur's efforts to unlawfully wield the family's monopoly power, for Arthur cast a giant shadow on Bill's life. As Bill himself is ever fond of saying, "I learned everything from him [Arthur], all elements of the business,"[1] including, it is now clear, the ruthless exploitation of the family's financial and political power.[2]

Since the Wirtz family's power has always rested in its control of the major sports stadiums throughout the country, Arthur Wirtz's rise to promi-

---

[1]Mike Kiley, "NHL Owners Love Wirtz Even If Hawks Fans Don't," *Chicago Tribune*, January 18, 1991, p. 3c.

[2]I have summarized the essential facts of the case here, but interested readers with no social life can find the courts' full opinions at *United States v. International Boxing Club*, 348 U.S. 236, 75 S.Ct. 259, 99 L.Ed. 290. (1955); *United States v. International Boxing Club*, 150 F. Supp. 397 (S.D.N.Y. 1957); *United States v. International Boxing Club*, 171 F. Supp. 841 (S.D.N.Y. 1957); and *United States v. International Boxing Club*, 358 U.S. 242; 79 S. Ct. 245; 3 L. Ed. 2d 270 (1959).

nence must be recounted. There has always been much mystery as to Arthur Wirtz's meteoric rise to great wealth and much speculation about the actual source of his money. The factual details of his early years are surprisingly sparse, but the accepted Horatio Alger storyline about Arthur's rise to wealth and power goes like this: Born in 1901, the son of a Chicago cop, Arthur Wirtz upon graduating from the University of Michigan in 1922 formed a real estate brokerage firm with two partners. The firm of Wirtz, Hubert and Little rapidly came to own or manage some 80 buildings in Chicago, with a total of 3,000 rental units on the city's lakefront, many of which the Wirtz family owns to this day. In 1933, at the age of thirty-two, Arthur met James Norris, Sr., a transplanted Canadian and multimillionaire speculator at the Chicago Board of Trade. Wirtz and Norris formed a real-estate partnership to buy up depressed properties.

It did not take long for the ambitious pair to become controlling forces in the indoor sports arena business and the NHL. The Canadian Norris had always pined to own an NHL team, and in 1933, taking full advantage of the Great Depression, the pair bought the Olympia Arena in Detroit and the Detroit Red Wings at fire-sale prices, paying ten-cents on the dollar.[3] In 1935, they bought the Chicago Stadium, paying $300,000 for the property that had been built six years earlier at a cost of $7 million. Over the next twenty years, Wirtz and Norris would also come to own 53 percent of Madison Square Garden and 100 percent of the St. Louis Arena, as well as exclusive leases for arenas in Omaha and Indianapolis.

In 1946, the trio of Norris Sr, his son, Jim Norris, Jr., and Arthur Wirtz purchased the Chicago Blackhawks, though they did so through a third party, thus avoiding the appearance of a conflict of interest with their ownership of the Red Wings. In 1954, the Norrises and the Wirtzes publicly assumed control of Blackhawks when, soon after the elder Norris died, a deal was struck between his two sons, Bruce Norris and Jim Norris, Jr., in which Bruce assumed control of the Red Wings and shares in Norris Grain Company while Jim, in partnership with the Wirtzes, retained the family's holding in the Blackhawks and the Chicago Stadium.

For almost four decades, Jim Norris, Jr. and Arthur Wirtz were the sultans of the NHL, though ironically Arthur himself was never much of a hockey person — indeed he was never much of sports person. As a close friend of Arthur's once put it, "He never really had any goals besides making a lot of money. Other rich guys with pro sports teams love to fraternize with their

---

[3]In 1927, the Detroit Olympia had been built for $2.5 million. Wirtz and Norris bought it for $250,000 and paid another $100,000 to purchase the Red Wings.

players and that sort of thing, but not him. He doesn't even especially care for sports. He gets his jollies from seeing a good bottom line."[4] The Norris/Wirtz duo was the dominant influence in hockey for decades, owning three of the six NHL teams at one time. New York columnist Dan Parker once famously quipped, "NHL meant Norris House League."

HOLD ON TO YOUR HAT, DON KING!

Having control over the Detroit Olympia, the Chicago Stadium, the St. Louis Arena, and other smaller stadiums, Wirtz and Norris were now in position to exploit their power to become the exclusive promoters and exhibitors of professional boxing in the United States. In 1949, the two men formed International Boxing Club (IBC) for the purpose of promoting and exhibiting boxing events.[5] Soon after its formation, IBC placed under exclusive contract the leading contenders in every principal division. From 1950-1959, IBC had control over virtually every championship fight in the country.[6] As the U.S. Supreme Court put it, IBC came to obtain an "odorous monopoly" that was "known and...feared in the boxing world."[7]

---

[4]Don Kowet, *The Rich Who Own Sports*, Random House, 1977, p. 191.

[5]Their business of promoting professional boxing grew out of an initial agreement with heavyweight champion Joe Louis. In 1949, then heavyweight champ Louis wanted to retire. One of Louis' managers, Truman Gibson, concocted a money-making scheme whereby Louis would obtain the promotional rights to all four of the leading heavyweight contenders — Ezzard Charles, Joe Walcott, Lee Savold, and Gus Lesnevich. This would allow Louis and his managers to arrange a so-called "elimination contest" among the four to replace Louis as the heavyweight champ. After securing these contracts, including the exclusive rights to radio, television and movie revenues of the fights, Gibson then assigned all four contracts to Wirtz and Norris' International Boxing Club, which paid Louis $150,000 cash, plus an employment contract, plus a 20 percent stock interest in IBC. At some point thereafter, Louis ceased to be a stockholder in IBC and his share was split evenly between Norris and Wirtz and Madison Square Garden. See 358 U.S. 242 at 245. The original IBC grew into a network of IBC's — e.g., the IBC of Illinois, the IBC of New York, the IBC of Michigan, and IBC of Missouri. Wirtz and Norris controlled all of them.

[6]How complete was IBC's control over championship boxing in the U.S.? From June 16, 1949 until May 15, 1953, when the first charges by the U.S. Justice Department were filed against them, there were 44 professional world championship bouts in the U.S., and Wirtz and Norris controlled the promotion of 36 of them. And in the other eight fights, they still had substantial financial interests, including exclusive television rights. In the two most popular weight divisions — heavyweight and middleweight — they controlled every single championship bout. Similarly, for the period January 1, 1951 until May 15, 1953, Wirtz and Norris controlled 25 out of 27 of the championship bouts in the country. And from May 16, 1953 until January 12, 1959, there were 37 championship bouts, and Wirtz and Norris totally controlled 24 of them and had financial interests in all 13 of the others.

[7]*Id.* at 254.

But why an "odorous monopoly"? And why a "feared" monopoly? There is no crime in obtaining a lawful monopoly, but at the trial held in 1957 brought against Wirtz and Norris by the U.S. Justice Department, the government established that the practices employed by Wirtz and Norris to attain their monopoly included conspiracy, blackmail, and extortion. And Congressional Hearings in 1959 and 1960, headed by Senator Estes Kefauver (hearings ever since known as the Kefauver Hearings), whose purpose was to cast light upon the rampant corruption in the U.S. boxing industry, revealed the close connections between Wirtz and Norris' companies, organized crime, acts of violence, bribery, illegal payoffs, and phony bookkeeping. The particular activities Wirtz and Norris engaged in to foster their illegal monopoly included the following:

Conspiracy: To eliminate all competition in the promotion of championship boxing, the court found that IBC had forged a conspiracy with its only competitor, Madison Square Garden. An agreement with the Garden effectively meant Wirtz and Norris would have no competition for the promotion of professional boxing.[8] New York City was the most important site in the country for the staging of championship boxing, and Madison Square Garden was the most important spot in New York. From 1937 through 1948, about 45 percent of all championship bouts presented in the United States were held in New York City and of those 75 percent were held at Madison Square Garden. The Garden's facilities were controlled by an exclusive lease with boxing promoter Mike Jacobs and his company, Twentieth Century Sporting Club. Twentieth Century Sporting Club was the leading boxing promoter of the day. Jacobs had an exclusive deal with the Garden whereby he and the Garden's owners shared 50-50 in the profits of all boxing contests held there.

In an effort to squeeze out Jacobs and Twentieth Century Sporting Club, on March 13, 1949, Arthur Wirtz wrote a letter to the president of Madison Square Garden proposing that Wirtz, Norris, and the owners of the Garden, "should work together now and keep the events for our buildings and not create a competitive situation that would be harmful to all."[9] By mid-April, the Garden agreed to break its lease with Jacobs and work exclusively with Wirtz and Norris to promote boxing events. Soon thereafter, Wirtz and Norris purchased 53 percent of the Garden stock, putting themselves in the position, as the Supreme Court explained, "to dictate its policies and boxing activities."[10] As a result of the agreement, the District Court explained, "all other promot-

---

[8] 150 F. Supp. 397 at 417.
[9] *Id.* at 413.
[10] 358 U.S. 242 at 248.

ers have been excluded from promoting championship contests."[11]

Blackmail: Wirtz and Norris were determined to make their stranglehold on the sport of boxing unbreakable. To do so, they instituted a policy requiring all fighters to sign exclusive contracts. In order to get a shot at a championship fight, IBC required all contenders to sign a contract stating that, if the contender won, "the contender would be employed exclusively by the defendants in all his matches, or in all matches of defense of his title, for a period of three years."[12] The effect of these contracts was, as the U.S. Supreme Court put it, simple blackmail: "the choice given a contender thereafter was clear, i.e., to sign with appellants [Wirtz and Norris] or not to fight."[13]

Extortion: From June 16, 1949 until May 15, 1953, there was only one time in which Wirtz and Norris did not have a promotional interest in a championship fight. Their company permitted another promoter, Dewey Michaels, of Buffalo, New York, to promote the contest. This was done, however, on the condition that Michaels agree to pay five percent of all monies received from the sale of tickets, and radio, television, and motion picture rights to them. Michaels refused to pay the five percent "juice" and in response Wirtz and Norris threatened to exclude Michaels from any future boxing contests in which the IBC was involved.[14]

The normally restrained Supreme Court rarely personalizes its decisions, but in this case the Court was so appalled by Wirtz and Norris' strong-arm tactics and disregard for the law that it could not help but express shock over their arrogance. The Court condemned Wirtz and Norris for continually thumbing their nose at the law:

> [S]ome two and a half years after our opinion in the former appeal on January 31, 1955, *it appears that appellants had continued exercising their unlawful control long after they well knew that this activity was within the coverage of the Sherman Act.* In view of the fact that no denial was made on that appeal of the sufficiency of the Government's complaint *it is reasonable to assume that appellants...knew that their conduct violated the Sherman Act, obedience to which is so important to our free enterprise system. Still they continued their illegal activity.* In fact from all appearances it is continuing to this day.[15] (Emphasis added.)

[11] 150 F. Supp. 397 at 417.

[12] *Id.* at 418.

[13] U.S. 242 at 248.

[14] 150 F. Supp. 397 at 418-419.

[15] 358 U.S. 242 at 258. This would not be the last time a court would be appalled by the

A KNOCK-OUT PUNCH

Determined to "cure the ill effects of the illegal conduct and assure the public freedom from its continuance," in 1957 the U.S. Supreme Court ordered Wirtz and Norris to sell all the stock they owned — 53 percent — in Madison Square Garden within a five year period. It also ordered the dissolution of their two largest boxing companies and ordered Wirtz and Norris to lease buildings controlled by them to other promoters. Additionally, it prohibited exclusive contracts applying to all professional boxing matches. The penalties imposed by the court effectively ended Wirtz and Norris' involvement with professional boxing.[16]

WIRTZ AND NORRIS' MOB TIES—
A HIGH 'CARBO' DIET

In addition to the Court's forced dissolution of Wirtz and Norris' companies, the Kefauver Hearings exposed IBC's role as a main player in the seedy underworld of professional boxing. In order to understand the illicit nature of Wirtz and Norris' actions, it's necessary to understand that since at least the time of Prohibition in the 1920s, boxing was the red-light district of professional sports — gangsters ran fighters, promoted fights, fixed fights and bet on fights. The world of boxing was a cesspool of violence and corruption. And the mob influence was especially strong when Wirtz and Norris ran things after World War II. As boxing historian David Remnick has put it, "After the war there was not a single champion who was not, in some way, touched by the Mafia, if not wholly owned and operated by it."[17] In 1949, the major player in the boxing world was a man named Frankie Carbo (a.k.a. Frank Fortunato, Frank Martin, Jimmy the Wop, Dago Frank, and the Ambassador). Born in 1904 in New York's lower East Side, Carbo was a lifelong gangster, arrested at 18 for assault and grand larceny, and at age 20 charged with shooting a butcher to death in a poolhall on East 160th. The two were arguing over who controlled possession of a stolen taxi cab. Convicted

---

Wirtzes' disregard for the law. As will be seen in Chapter Two, in *Fishman v. Wirtz*, 1981 U.S. Dist. Lexis 9998, (October 28, 1981), the judge called Arthur and Bill Wirtz everything but serial perjurers.

[16]This is only a summary of the penalties imposed on Wirtz and Norris. For a full recitation, see 358 U.S. 242 at 354-356.

[17]David Remnick, *King of The World: Muhammad Ali and The Rise of An American Hero*, Random House, New York, 1998 p. 46. I am indebted to this book for a clear understanding of the connection between the Mafia and Wirtz and Norris' companies. Though Remnick's book is primarily a biography of the early career of Muhammad Ali, the book also provides an excellent history of the corrupt practices that riddled professional boxing in the 1930s, 40s, and 50s.

of first degree murder, Carbo spent five years in prison, until he was paroled in 1930.[18]

Upon his release, amidst the Prohibition wars, Carbo became a trigger-man for the Brooklyn Division of the notorious Murder Incorporated, committing and escaping murder charges with the uncanny ease of someone who had friends in all the right places. On April 12, 1933, for example, Max Hassel and Max Greenberg, two henchmen aligned with the liquor baron known as Waxie Gordon, were found shot dead at the Hotel Carteret in Elizabeth, New Jersey. Several witnesses fingered Carbo, who was charged with the killing, but after being released on ten thousand dollars bail nothing else came of the investigation.

Then, on Thanksgiving Eve in 1939, mobster Harry "Big Greenie" Greenberg was found dead, with five bullets in him, sitting behind the wheel of his car. The grand jury handed down indictments against Carbo as the trig-german, Bugsy Siegel, the driver of the getaway car, and Emanuel "Mendy" Weiss and Louis Lepke, as accomplices. Though eye-witnesses said they saw Carbo running away from the scene of the crime, that eye-witness mysteriously sailed out of his window and down five stories to his death while under police guard at the Half Moon Hotel in Coney Island. Without an eye-witness, the jury acquitted Carbo of the murder.[19]

By 1949, it was Carbo who controlled boxing throughout the United States, so much so that in the years after World War II until he was arrested in 1959, Carbo was known as the "underworld commissioner."[20] His power worked like this: Through violence and threats of violence, he would install shadow managers (men like Herman "Hymie the Mink" Wallman, Willie "The Undertaker" Ketchum, Al "The Vest" Weill, Joseph "Pep" Barone) and then took a piece of the action. If a fighter refused to go along, he had a hard time finding fights, much less title fights. The penalty for non-compliance was savage and inevitable. Carbo left nothing to chance. He personally offered to gouge out the eyes of one West Coast promoter who resisted him. As Remnick explained, "[Carbo] single-handedly controlled the lightweight, welterweight, and middleweight titles for twenty years as he kept a grip on

---

[18]*Id.* at 59.

[19]Mob lore also has it that in 1947 it was Frankie Carbo who killed Bugsy Siegel, the visionary founder of the Flamingo Hotel in Las Vegas. The famous mafia snitch Jimmy Frattianno said that Carbo was directed to kill Siegel after Siegel failed to pay debts he owed to the mob. *Id.*

[20]*Id.* at 60. As Remnick explained: "Carbo did not invent the mafia way of running fighters, but he did refine the details and established such a dominance in the field that especially in the years after World War II until his arrest in 1959, he was known as the 'underworld commissioner.'"

such champions as Joe Brown, Jimmy Carter, Virgil Akins, Johnny Sexton, Kid Gavilan, Carmon Basilio, Sugar Ray Robinson, Jake LaMotta, and Sonny Liston...Rather than add up the fighters he controlled, a better exercise would be to find the few he did not."[21]

And who was Carbo's most important connection within the boxing world? James Norris, Jr. IBC's success was intimately connected with its association and payoffs to Frankie Carbo. The association of Wirtz and Norris and Carbo allowed IBC to gain control over top fighters in every division. Wirtz and Norris hardly made a match without Carbo's approval, and whenever Norris needed help to complete a fight, he'd call his friend, Frankie. Carbo and IBC were unquestionably a perfect fit. The two needed and depended on each other. As the Kefauver's Committee congressional counsel Jack Bonhomie explained, there was no mystery as to why they were in bed together: "Norris and Carbo got close because Norris had Madison Square Garden and Chicago Stadium and all the money, and Carbo had the fighters and the managers in his pocket. They needed each other, and together they had absolute power over boxing."[22]

Similarly, Jack Kearns, a boxing professional for over 60 years, the manager of heavyweight champ Jack Dempsey, a man with well-known ties to the mob himself, told the Kefauver Commission: "There is no doubt about it. Norris and Carbo run everything in boxing, and when they feel like it they throw you a bone once in a while."[23] Likewise, Truman Gibson, a Chicago attorney, the former manager to Joe Louis, a man who was actively involved

---

[21]*Id.* at 61-62. One well-known victim of Carbo's rage was the legendary fight manager, Ray Arcel, who died in 1994 at 94 years old. In the course of his career in boxing from the 1920s to the 1980s, Arcel trained 18 world champions, the last being Roberto ("The Hands of Stone") Duran. Arcel was Duran's trainer that fateful night in 1980 when Duran at 2:44 of the eighth round quit in his rematch against Sugar Ray Leonard, with the infamous words, "No mas, no mas." Back in the 1950s, Arcel was a wayward Carbo-controlled manager who had asserted his independence and was rewarded with a lead-pipe thrashing that almost killed him. Carbo's "technique" was as follows: "See what they do, they use a water pipe, see, you know, regular lead water pipe. Lead pipe. And about that short. About that thick. And they just get an ordinary piece of newspaper, see, newspaper don't show fingerprints. Then they take it and they wrap it just in the newspaper, see, just an ordinary piece of paper, that's all they ever use...they whack you twice and split your — fracture your skull, and knock you unconscious." See *Paul John Carbo, et al v. United States of America*, 314 F.2d 718, 729 (Ninth Cir. 1963).

[22]Remnick at 61.

[23]U.S. Senate Committee on the Judiciary. Subcommittee on Antitrust and Monopoly. *Professional Boxing* Hearings, December 5-9, 12-14, 1960. Testimony of Jack Kearns, p. 492. Washington: Government Printing Office, 1961. (Hereinafter cited as "Kefauver Hearings.")

in the daily affairs of the Wirtz and Norris' International Boxing Clubs, at one point even acting as the corporation's president, acknowledged that IBC had sustained dealings with the underworld in order "to maintain a free flow of fighters without interference, without strikes, without sudden illnesses, without sudden postponements" and to insure that no one caused international boxing any, as Gibson put it, "trouble."[24]

Carbo made money through his contracts with the fighters. A typical contract was future heavyweight champ Sonny Liston's. The five-year contract with his "manager" Joseph "Pep" Barone — a front man for Carbo — entitled Barone to 50 percent of Liston's income. But an unwritten clause in the contract delivered most of that percentage to Carbo, with only a small piece going to Barone himself.[25] Carbo also made money through undisclosed payoffs to him by the IBC. In 1960, during the Kefauver Hearings, it was exposed that Carbo's girlfriend (later wife), Viola Masters, was employed on IBC's payroll and received $40,000 over three years. Under oath, Truman Gibson was asked what duties she performed. He answered "none." He explained that she was on the payroll to buy Frankie Carbo's "good will."[26] Asked why IBC hired Mrs. Carbo instead of Frankie Carbo, Truman Gibson said, "Because it looked a little bit better on our records, not ever considering the possibility of being called before a Senate investigative committee, to have Viola Masters down instead of Frank Carbo."[27]

In short, during the heyday of Wirtz and Norris' power in boxing, the business of boxing was thoroughly corrupt, and it is indisputable that Wirtz and Norris were intimately involved in that corruption. Indeed, the most damning testament to IBC and the mob's relationship in the world of boxing doesn't come from court records or the findings of the Kefauver Commission. Instead, it comes from an offhand remark by one of the mobsters themselves. There was a dinner sometime in 1957-1958 where mobster Frankie Carbo regularly held court with his managers and various other flackies. By this point, Carbo's organization was deteriorating, and the U.S.

---

[24]Kefauver Hearings at 492.

[25]Nick Tosches, "The Outlaw Champ," *Vanity Fair*, February, 1998, p. 162.

[26]Kefauver Hearings at 334.

[27]Senator Kefauver replied, "That is an honest answer." In contrast to Gibson's honesty, when asked under oath if the purpose of hiring Viola Masters was "to create good influence and goodwill with Frankie Carbo," Jim Norris waffled painfully, saying: "I definitely admit that it looks that way, and possibly unconsciously I had that in mind. But I really did think that she might be able to possibly with a little extra effort on Carbo's part plus her own, I am sure — I thought she was an attractive lady — with other managers might have someway of helping that a man wouldn't have, just by graciousness, you know, just being a girl." *Id.* at 559.

Supreme Court had already ordered the IBC dismantled. But undercover agents were still accumulating evidence against IBC and Frankie Carbo's operation, and they had infiltrated Carbo's mob meetings. At this particular mob dinner, Blinky Palermo, Carbo's right-hand man and the "shadow" manager of Sonny Liston, announced in despair, "The trouble with boxing today is that legitimate businessmen are horning in on our game,"[28] meaning the good ol' days of the Wirtz-Norris-Carbo Era were drawing to a close.

A LESSON LEARNED WELL — TOO DAMN WELL

The scoundrel of the IBC episode has always been assumed to be Norris, not Wirtz. Norris was the one who hobnobbed with Carbo and his mob friends. Norris was the one who was brought before the Kefauver Commission. Wirtz never even had to testify before Congress about his involvement in the IBC. But it strains credulity to believe Wirtz was ignorant of the mob connections, mob tactics, illegal payoffs, and the phony book-keeping. First, it is widely understood that, business-wise, Jim Norris, Jr. did very little without Arthur's approval. According to a business associate, "Jim rarely made a move without clearing it with Arthur."[29] As Norris himself testified under oath at the Kefauver Hearings, it was Arthur, and Arthur alone, who controlled the IBC's books: "[Regarding financial matters], I have the utmost confidence in my partner, and that is his department and his job."[30] In addition, Norris testified that he always took a back seat to Arthur in business matters: "I don't question what he does in situations like that [corporate finances] any more than he would question me what I did with a hockey player."[31]

Second, there is strong evidence that connects Wirtz to the illegal mob payoffs. When asked under oath at the Kefauver Hearings who had to approve all phony payments made to Mrs. Carbo, Truman Gibson made it clear that Arthur Wirtz had "to OK the payments."[32] Moreover, Mrs. Frankie Carbo wasn't the only dubious figure on the Wirtz and Norris payroll. A man named Max Courtney (a.k.a. "Max Schmertzler") was also found to have been paid $76,000 over three years for no apparent work.[33] According to Norris' testimony, Mr. Courtney was "hire[d]" by "and reported" to Mr.

---

[28]Remnick at 63.

[29]Kowet, *The Rich Who Own Sports* at 187.

[30]Kefauver Hearings at 579.

[31]*Id.* at 577.

[32]*Id.* at 331.

[33]Sounds suspiciously like Bob Pulford's current management arrangement with the Blackhawks.

Wirtz.[34] Kefauver Committee testimony also disclosed that mob-connected payments were made to Jack Kearns in the amount of $140,000, not for any explicit work done, but solely for Mr. Kearn's "goodwill" and "to ease...problems [IBC] was faced with."[35]

Third, Arthur Wirtz was famous for being a stickler for details. For him to be ignorant of illegal payoffs to mobsters and phony bookkeeping was contrary to his nature. His nickname was not the "Baron of the Bottom Line" for nothing. He had an obsessive work ethic, with concentrated focus on day-to-day business and bookkeeping matters. According to one close friend, "We kidded him that his [first two] initials, A.M., stood for 'After Midnight,' because he'd wake up guys at three in the morning to talk business."[36]

Yet despite all the evidence tying Arthur Wirtz to the mob, the point here is not that Arthur Wirtz was himself a mobster. His defenders will tell you that he was merely a prudent businessman who utilized the services of the mob, made illegal payoffs to them, and profited enormously from the violence and intimidation engaged in by the mob. They will point out that Arthur Wirtz was not alone in doing this and that the 1930s, 40s, and 50s had a different ethos when it came to such business practices. And they will argue that these actions occurred almost 50 years ago now and should be dismissed as nothing more than ancient history.

And to a large extent they are correct.

But, sadly, viewed in the context of Bill Wirtz's professional career, these illegal activities are more accurately seen as a prologue of what was to come, as a foreshadowing of the type of shady commercial behavior that Bill Wirtz himself would engage in repeatedly, and as blueprint for a man willing to suppress serious scruples in the name of profit.

---

[34]Norris testified that Norris and Wirtz paid $2,000 a month for three years to Mr. Courtney to sell "boxing photos" to various media outlets, but in three years Mr. Courtney sold just three photos. Explaining why he sold only three photos, Norris told the Committee, "I think we were just a little bit ahead of that market." *Id*. at 578-579.

[35]*Id*. at 579.

[36]Kowet, *The Rich Who Own Sports* at 191.

"Competition? Gentleman, that's the one
thing about capitalism that I can do without!"

CHAPTER 2

The Illegal Use Of Monopoly Power To Buy the Chicago Bulls

*"If you can build a business big enough,
it's respectable."*

— *Will Rogers*

In 1972, just 13 years after Arthur Wirtz had been denounced by the U.S. Supreme Court for violating the antitrust laws in the world of professional boxing, the Wirtzes again violated the antitrust laws. The story involves a series of underhanded, covert actions undertaken by both Arthur and Bill to prevent a Milwaukee man, Marvin Fishman, from purchasing the Bulls for $3.3 million so that the Wirtzes could purchase the team instead. A U.S. District Court found that Arthur and Bill's efforts to purchase the Bulls were not honestly industrial and had nothing to do with business skill, acumen, or fair, competitive conduct, but were merely the result of exclusionary, predatory, anticompetitive and illegal acts that stemmed from their ability to exploit their monopoly power.[1] One District Court judge succinctly dubbed the Wirtzes' actions here a "shabby story of economic blackmail."[2]

---

[1] See *Fishman v. Wirtz et al.*, 1981 U.S. Dist. Lexis 9998 at 106 (October 28, 1981). Fishman's legal battle against the Wirtzes lasted for over 12 years. The case was originally filed in 1974; trial was held in 1979; and the appellate court's decision affirming the trial court's ruling was decided in 1986. The various courts' opinions and findings of fact in this case can be found at *Fishman v. Wirtz, et al.*, 1981 U.S. Dist. Lexis 9998 at 106 (October 28, 1981); *Fishman v. Estate of Arthur Wirtz, et al.*, 594 F. Supp. 853 (1984); and *Fishman v. Estate of Arthur Wirtz, et al.*, 807 F.2d 520 (7th Cir. 1986).

[2] *Chicago Stadium Corporation v. United States of America*, 1991 U.S. Dist. Lexis 9047 (June 24, 1991).

Their shabby efforts resulted in a $12.4 million judgment against them and their co-conspirators, plus punitive damages of $2.5 million dollars and attorneys' fees totaling over $4 million.[3]

CHICAGO'S FINEST

In 1966, the NBA awarded an expansion franchise — the Chicago Bulls — to Elmer Rich and his company. By 1971, Rich was looking to sell the team. In 1972, it became clear that two groups were competing to purchase the team. One of the groups was led by Marvin Fishman, a Milwaukee resident involved in the real estate business who had a small interest in the Milwaukee Bucks. The other group was led by Lester Crown and Arthur Wirtz and consisted of a group of prominent (mostly) Chicago businessmen, including real-estate developer Philip Klutznick (former Ambassador to the United Nations under Richard Nixon), James Cook (retired president and chief executive officer of Illinois Bell Telephone Company), Bill Wirtz and a relative unknown named George Steinbrenner (a Cleveland shipping magnate, who in 1974 would go on to purchase some New York baseball team whose name escapes us). The entity formed to purchase the Bulls by this group was called Chicago Professional Sports Corporation, which will be referred to here as the Wirtz group.

In 1972, both parties bid $3.3 million for the team, but based on the firmness and merits of the respective offers, Rich chose to sell the team to the Fishman group, concluding that certain "ambiguous" terms of the Wirtz group's offer made the Fishman group's offer superior.[4] On June 2, 1972 Fishman's attorney submitted a signed offer to purchase the Bulls, and that same day Bulls' owner Elmer Rich wrote a letter to Arthur Wirtz advising him that the Bulls' had accepted Fishman's offer because Fishman had agreed to pay all cash at closing. On June 14, 1972, Fishman's group and the Bulls' ownership signed a written agreement to purchase the Bulls for $3.3 million. With the signing of the agreement, it could be said, as the District Court did say, that "Fishman had successfully won the competition [to purchase the Bulls] by making an offer to purchase which the Bulls' owners found acceptable and accepted."[5]

---

[3]See *Fishman v. Wirtz, et al.*, 594 F. Supp. 853 at 892.

[4]Bulls owner Elmer Rich explained at trial that "[The Fishman group's] contract and offer was [sic] perceived by the Bulls to be preferable to [the Wirtz group's] offer for several reasons, among them was the fact that various ambiguities and problems in the [Wirtz group's] offer would require additional negotiations." *Id*. at 526.

[5]*Fishman v. Wirtz, et al.*, 1981 U.S. Dist. Lexis 9998 at 6.

With the papers signed, everything was set for approval by the league at the NBA's Board of Governors meeting in June of 1972. Under NBA by-laws, in order for ownership of a team to be transferred, a three-quarter vote is needed by the NBA Board of Governors. In 1972, there were seventeen NBA teams. Three-quarters meant 13 affirmative votes were needed.[6]

There was just one problem. Smarting from Elmer Rich's decision to accept the Fishman offer over their own, Arthur and Bill Wirtz were determined to interfere with the sale. The Wirtzes forged a twofold strategy to prevent Fishman from buying the Bulls. First, Bill and Arthur set about to organize a conspiracy among certain NBA owners to vote against league approval of the Fishman group by lobbying "friendly" NBA owners to vote against the transfer of the Bulls. The Wirtzes only needed to win five votes to foil the transaction. It was the Wirtzes' ace in the hole that several NBA owners also happened to own NHL teams and thus were beholden to the Wirtzes, who at the time were among the two most powerful men in hockey. Second, the Wirtzes refused to negotiate in good faith with the Fishman group for a lease at the Wirtz-owned Chicago Stadium, so that even if the Bulls were eventually purchased by the Fishman group, the team would have no place to play their home games. The NBA viewed the Chicago Stadium as the only arena in Chicago acceptable for the Bulls. Since the Wirtzes controlled access to the Stadium, their refusal to negotiate a lease with Fishman, or any other group for that matter, meant they could hold the sale of the Bulls hostage, which is exactly what they did.

FILET O' FISHMAN

The Wirtz group's effort to lobby the NBA owners against the transfer of the Bulls to the Fishman group began in earnest on June 12, 1972. On that day, several of the investors in the Wirtz group sent a telegram to the NBA commissioner and the NBA Board of Governors advising them that the Wirtz group was sending yet another offer to the Bulls that increased their previous offer by $50,000, thereby making their offer larger than any other offer to purchase the Bulls. This letter was sent despite Bulls owner Elmer Rich's previous rejection of the Wirtz group's offer and despite the existence of a valid, signed purchase agreement between Rich and the Fishman group. The telegram stated that this offer would comply with all the terms and conditions

---

[6]In 1972, the NBA was composed of the following 17 teams: Atlanta Hawks, Baltimore Bullets, Boston Celtics, Buffalo Braves, Chicago Bulls, Cincinnati Royals, Cleveland Cavaliers, Detroit Pistons, Golden State Warriors, Houston Rockets, Los Angeles Lakers, Milwaukee Bucks, New York Knicks, Philadelphia 76ers, Phoenix Suns, Portland Trailblazers and Seattle Supersonics.

required by the Bulls' owners. The telegram stated further:

> Our responsible group, principally composed of Chicagoans, includes Albert Adelman, James Cook, Lester Crown, Edward Ginsberg, Philip M. Klutznick, Arnold R. Meyer, George M. Steinbrenner III, and Arthur Wirtz. We have reached an agreement with Arthur Wirtz owner of the Chicago Stadium for a ten year lease *which insures the availability to us of the best arena with the largest seating capacity in Chicago at which the Chicago Bowls [sic] can play.*[7] (Emphasis added.)

The purpose of the telegram was to alert the NBA owners that the Wirtzes were determined to hold Chicago Stadium hostage so that nobody other than the Wirtz group would be allowed to play home games there.[8]

To interfere further with Fishman's plans to purchase the Bulls, on June 13th, the Wirtz group sent its president, James Cook, and its attorney, Robert Merritt, to the NBA Board of Governors meeting in Virginia, where the vote on the transfer of the Bulls was to occur. The Wirtz group had no scheduled business before the NBA for consideration at the meeting, and the NBA had requested no information from or about the Wirtz group. Cook and Merritt went to the Virginia NBA meeting solely to lobby against and undermine the sale of the Bulls to Fishman.

On June 15th, Bulls' owner Elmer Rich presented the proposed transfer of the Chicago franchise to the NBA Board of Governors for approval. By permitting the issue to be put to a vote, NBA Commissioner Walter Kennedy indicated that from his perspective the transfer was in order. In addition, the NBA Commissioner's office and the NBA Finance Committee had investigated the Fishman group and had approved their financial and moral ability and fitness to own the Bulls. Yet when the matter was put to a vote, seven of the 17 NBA members voted to not approve the transfer.

Two reasons for the rejection were given: (1) Fishman did not have a lease and, specifically, did not have a lease at the Chicago Stadium; and (2) certain NBA owners said that they preferred that the Wirtz group purchase the Bulls from the Rich group instead of the Fishman group. As to the lease situation, Bulls' owner Rich told the governors that he believed a lease at the

---

[7]*Fishman v. Wirtz et al.*, 1981 U.S. Dist. Lexis 9998 at 27.

[8]Trial transcript, Case No. 74 C 2814, p. 1055-56 and p. 288-290. Both Lester Crown and James Cook testified under oath that they intended that this telegram would result in a rejection of the Fishman contract.

Chicago Stadium would be available to Fishman, and, if for some reason it was not, the International Amphitheater might be available. As for the Wirtz group's interest in purchasing the team, Rich told the NBA that he had *never* received what he considered to be an acceptable offer from them.

Immediately after the unfavorable vote, Rich stomped out of the NBA meeting room. Someone then suggested that, since the primary problem raised was the lack of a lease, the negative vote be rescinded to allow Rich to secure a lease commitment. The proposed transfer could then be presented for another vote at the next NBA meeting to be held in New York in July. This proposal was adopted, and Rich was so informed. Several NBA members told Rich that a lease would be absolutely necessary to obtain NBA approval of the Bulls' transfer.

IT'S MY STADIUM —
AND I'LL MONOPOLIZE IT IF I WANT TO

After being told that a lease would be necessary to obtain approval from the NBA, Bulls' owner Elmer Rich and owner-in-waiting Marvin Fishman discussed plans for approaching Arthur Wirtz about a lease at the Chicago Stadium. The two decided that Rich and his attorney would attempt to meet with Arthur Wirtz, and that Fishman should independently attempt to arrange a meeting with Wirtz.

On the following Monday, June 19th, and continuing until June 29th, Fishman attempted in vain to arrange a meeting with Arthur Wirtz to discuss a lease. Wirtz, however, refused to even speak to Fishman.[9]

Rich was able to meet face-to-face with Wirtz on June 21st, but his efforts to obtain a lease for the Fishman group were completely unsuccessful. Wirtz told Rich that he needed a guaranteed lease for 10 years from Rich if he sold the team to the Fishman group because of his "concern" about the financial responsibility of the Fishman group and their ability to pay the rent. Wirtz, however, had never even met with Fishman to learn about the group's financial stability and thus had no way of knowing the group's financial situation.

In addition to the unreasonable demand for a 10-year guaranteed lease, Wirtz asked Rich point-blank to sell the Bulls to his group or, in the alterna-

---

[9]Specifically, Fishman telephoned Wirtz on June 19th and was told that Wirtz was not in. Fishman explained to Wirtz's secretary that he wanted to schedule a meeting to discuss a lease and requested that Wirtz return his call. Wirtz did not respond. On June 22nd and 26th, Fishman again telephoned Wirtz and left the same message, and again Wirtz did not respond. Finally, on June 28th, Fishman sent a telegram to Wirtz requesting a meeting. Wirtz responded by letter of June 29th stating, "there is no point of a meeting." *Fishman v. Wirtz et al.*, 1981 U.S. Dist. Lexis 9998, 38 (October 28, 1981).

tive, to present both offers to the NBA Board of Governors and allow the Board to choose. Rich told Wirtz that a sale to the Wirtz group was out of the question because of the contract already entered into with the Fishman group. Fishman requested that Wirtz put his 10-year lease proposal in writing.

On June 22nd and June 26th, Rich wrote Wirtz asking for the written lease proposal promised by Wirtz. On June 27th, Arthur Wirtz responded by letter to Rich. He did not enclose or discuss the 10-year lease, but instead insisted that the Bulls be sold to his group notwithstanding the fact that the Rich group had previously entered into a contract to sell to the Fishman group. In the letter, Wirtz made it clear that he believed that he, not Bulls' owner Elmer Rich, should determine to whom the Bulls should be sold. The letter read in part:

> We [the Wirtzes] and the league are the ones that should make the decision on who is the best acceptable tenant. If your present owners want to sell and would give me a firm cash price that is acceptable to you and your associates, that you indicated to the NBA at their league meeting was acceptable, I am sure I can get a very strong financially responsible group to buy your franchise and players and also a group that would be acceptable to us and to the League.[10] (Emphasis added.)

Arthur Wirtz sent copies of this letter to NBA Commissioner Walter Kennedy and Washington Bullets owner Abe Pollin, the NBA president. Bill Wirtz sent a copy of the letter to Los Angeles Lakers owner Jack Kent Cooke, along with a cover letter asking Cooke to call Bill Wirtz to discuss the matter. From this series of communications, the Wirtzes made it clear to the members of the NBA that Fishman did not, and would not, have a lease at the Chicago Stadium, but that the Wirtz group would have such a lease, and that the Wirtz group wanted to purchase the Bulls.

On June 29th, Rich met again in Arthur Wirtz's office with Arthur and Bill Wirtz. At this meeting, Arthur Wirtz reiterated his demand that the Bulls be sold to him and suggested ways that the proposed transfer to Fishman could be "handled" so as to assure its failure. There was no serious discussion at the meeting concerning a possible 10-year lease for the Fishman group. And as soon as Arthur Wirtz raised the question as to how the Bulls could be sold to him, Rich interjected that he was there only to discuss a lease for the Fishman group and that if the Wirtzes did not want to discuss that sub-

---

[10]*Fishman v. Wirtz et al.*, 1981 U.S. Dist. Lexis 9998 at 41.

ject, the conversation would have to stop.[11]

By mid-May, Marvin Fishman was aware that Arthur Wirtz was intent on interfering with his efforts to purchase the Bulls, and he realized that if he was going to prevail, he had to find an alternative place for the Bulls to play. On May 24th, Fishman telephoned a Chicago real estate broker and asked about alternative sites for the Bulls. He was told that the Chicago Amphitheater was the only other possible site. Fishman visited the Amphitheater on June 8th, and on July 5th, six days before the upcoming July 11th NBA meeting, and certain that Wirtz refused to make any sort of lease available at Chicago Stadium, Fishman executed a lease at the Amphitheater.

Meanwhile, the Wirtz group continued their clandestine efforts to organize support among NBA owners to reject the Fishman group's valid contract. Bill Wirtz discussed the status of the arena situation with Baltimore Bullets' owner Abe Pollin in early July 1972. On July 7th, Bill Wirtz wrote Pollin setting forth the limited and, according to Wirtz, inadequate seating capacity of the International Amphitheater. Also, Ed Ginsberg, a Cleveland attorney and member of the Wirtz group, sent a letter and telegram to the New York Knicks' head man Ned Irish. At the same time, Bill Wirtz called the Atlanta Hawks' owner Bill Putnam and informed him that the Wirtz group could obtain a lease at the Chicago Stadium, whereas Fishman could not. Arthur Wirtz called Houston Rockets' owner Ray Patterson to say the same thing. Additionally, the Bullets' Abe Pollin and the Knicks' Ned Irish telephoned Bulls' owner Rich and asked him what could be done to convince him to change his mind to sell the Bulls to the Wirtz group. The telegrams and letters and conversations sent by the Wirtz group to NBA members all made it clear that Chicago Stadium would be available to the Bulls only if the Bulls were sold to the Wirtz group.

I LOVE THIS (UNDERHANDED) GAME!

At the July 11, 1972 NBA meeting, Bulls owner Elmer Rich again requested the NBA Board of Governors approve the transfer of the Chicago franchise to the Fishman group. Rich explained that Arthur Wirtz would not lease Chicago Stadium to Fishman, and Fishman had instead arranged a lease at the International Amphitheater. Certain NBA governors openly expressed their desire to have the team sold by Rich to the Wirtz group, and after lim-

---

[11]Rich had been advised by his lawyers not to discuss the sale of the Bulls to the Wirtz group. It would have violated his signed purchase agreement with the Fishman group. A clause in the purchase agreement required Rich to use his "best efforts" to secure NBA approval of the transfer of the Bulls to Fishman. Discussion with Wirtz to undermine the Fishman contract would have violated Rich's duty to give his "best efforts." *Id.* at 42.

ited discussion and upon a vote, the proposed transfer to Fishman was denied. Thirteen affirmative votes were needed: Ten members voted to approve the transfer, seven members voted against it. The Wirtzes' hardball tactics had succeeded.

In looking at the teams that voted against the transfer, it is no surprise that they were almost all teams that were affiliated with the NHL — Atlanta, Los Angeles, New York, Baltimore, and Kansas City. At the time of the vote, the NBA's Atlanta Hawks were owned by William Putnam, the same man who owned the NHL's Atlanta Flames. The Los Angeles Lakers owner Jack Kent Cooke owned both the NBA's Lakers and the NHL's Los Angeles Kings. The New York Knicks and the NHL's Rangers were both owned by Madison Square Garden. The Kansas City Kings were owned in part by the Jacobs family, the same family which at the time owned Emprise Corp., which for decades had been the concessionaires at the Chicago Stadium.[12] And just prior to the July 11th vote denying the transfer of the Bulls, Baltimore Bullets owner Abe Pollin solicited and ultimately received the support of Arthur and Bill Wirtz in his attempt to acquire an expansion NHL franchise, the Washington Capitals. Pollin was granted an expansion team later in 1972, and the Washington Capitals entered the league in 1974. As the District Court in the case wrote, "Certainly, it is not mere coincidence that all of the NBA team owners who also owned NHL teams voted against [Fishman's group]. Nor is it a coincidence that the team which was owned by the concessionaire at the Chicago Stadium also voted against [the Fishman group]."[13]

The denial of NBA approval effectively ended Marvin Fishman's dream of acquiring the Bulls. On July 19, 1972, the Fishman contract was terminated. Shortly thereafter, the Bulls renewed negotiations to sell the team to the Wirtz group. Certain offers by both parties were considered and rejected until a contract was executed on July 28, 1972. And on August 10, 1972, the NBA approved the transfer of the Bulls to the Wirtz group.[14]

ARTHUR AND BILL'S $16.4 MILLION MISADVENTURE

It took Marvin Fishman 12 years of battling the Wirtzes in court, but in the end he won a judgment against them for $12.42 million in damages.

[12]The Jacobs family later went on to buy the Boston Bruins, which they own to this day.

[13]The other two "no" votes were Houston and Phoenix: Houston Rockets' owner Ray Patterson was an old friend of Arthur Wirtz, and Phoenix' governor, Robert Bloch, testified that he "had no present recollection" of why Phoenix voted against the transfer of the Bulls to the Fishman group. *Fishman v. Wirtz et al.*, 1981 U.S. Dist. Lexis 9998 at 167.

[14]Arthur and Bill Wirtz initially took a 16.9 percent equity position in the team and over the years increased their ownership interest to a little over 26 percent. See *Fishman v. Wirtz et al*, 594 F. Supp. at 874. The Wirtzes own a small piece of the Bulls to this day.

Fishman's attorneys were also awarded approximately $4 million in legal fees.[15] The court found the Wirtzes had illegally interfered with Fishman's contract to purchase the Bulls through exclusionary, unreasonable, anticompetitive means and ruled that the Wirtzes' refusal to negotiate a lease with the Fishman group illegally excluded the Fishman group from entering the professional basketball market in violation of the antitrust laws, thus enabling the Wirtzes and their co-conspirators to foreclose competition to acquire the Bulls and allowing them to obtain the team for themselves.[16]

But legal violations aside, what surprised the court most of all was the Wirtzes' complete lack of honesty, willful disregard for the truth, and arrogant contempt for the law. The judge condemned both men for their courtroom deceit, calling them everything but serial perjurers and deriding them for their "inconsistent opinions" and "lack of credibility:"

> In this court's opinion, it is astoundingly unbelievable that these very defendants [Bill and Arthur Wirtz], who pride themselves on being tough and competent businessmen had difficulty remembering the events surrounding their alleged competition aimed at obtaining the Bulls' franchise.[17]

The judge thought it absolutely remarkable that during their depositions prior to the trial the Wirtzes could not recall *any* of their efforts to manipulate the voting of the NBA owners. Bill Wirtz, for instance, didn't recall *any* of his communications concerning the transfer of the Bulls with William Putnam, Jack Kent Cooke, or Abe Pollin. Similarly, Arthur Wirtz couldn't recall *any* of his communications with Jack Kent Cooke, Ray Patterson, or any other NBA member. In fact, when Arthur was asked to explain the statement in his letter of November 8, 1972, to Lester Crown, reminding Crown that he and his son, Bill, were responsible for "lining up the [NBA] votes," Arthur claimed that he did not recall *anything* Bill had ever done in this matter.

Mocking the two for their 'situational amnesia,' the judge tartly observed that the Wirtzes changed their story at trial only after the facts became known and they could no longer deny with any semblance of plausibility their efforts to interfere with the NBA's voting. As the judge put it, "At trial, defendants' story was different — [but only] after plaintiff had garnered all the evidence."[18] He continued, "When defendants could no longer ignore the proof of their con-

[15]*Id.* at 892 (1984).
[16]*Fishman v. Wirtz et al* 1981 U.S. Dist. Lexis 9998 at 115 (October 28, 1981).
[17]*Id.* at 197.
[18]*Id.* at 197.

duct, they attempted to structure some 'justification' for it."[19] No longer able to deny their numerous conversations and correspondences with the members of the NBA's Board of Governors, the new 'theme' the Wirtzes presented to the court was that they weren't out to interfere in anybody's purchase agreement but were, gosh, simply calling on certain old friends to help persuade them to consider the Wirtz group as a potential NBA buyer. This new 'theme,' however, was totally at odds with the story they had previously told under oath. In general, it is not easy to impress a judge with one's lying. Judges, after all, spend a good deal of their time watching people manipulate and evade the truth. So for a judge to characterize the Wirtzes' testimony as "astoundingly unbelievable" indicates a degree of mendacity and falsification that surpasses your standard, garden-variety lying and deceit.

On top of the Wirtzes' allergy to the truth, it also came out at trial that both father and son enjoyed bragging about their lawless acts. In a letter of Nov. 8, 1972, to Lester Crown, Arthur Wirtz wrote:

> I believe my son, Bill, and I had a great deal to do with lining up the votes to make our deal possible, and this was on the second go-around after the first go-around had failed. This should indicate we are not exactly amateurs in this field.[20]

Here, at long last, Arthur Wirtz was telling the truth. (Quick, someone get a camera!) He and his son were certainly no "amateurs in this field." As shown in chapter one, Arthur had ample previous experience with using his monopoly power over the Stadium to illegally crush the economic rights of others.

Similarly, Bill himself bragged that the threat of ordinary legal sanction was not enough to make *him* obey the law. At the same time the Wirtzes were using Chicago Stadium as a weapon against the Fishman group, Bill announced that he would also withhold the Stadium from the newly formed World Hockey Association without regard to legal consequences. After being told by lawyers for the NHL that he was legally obligated to make Chicago Stadium available to a WHA team on fair and reasonable terms, Bill stated that the law held no sway over him. "Regardless of legal consequences," he asserted, "Chicago Stadium would not be leased to a WHA club."[21]

As punishment for lying under oath and contempt for the law, the court imposed punitive damages on Arthur and Bill of $2 million and $500,000,

---

[19]*Id.*at 197.
[20]*Id.* at 40, fn. 9.
[21]Trial transcript, case No. 74 C 2814, p. 481-482.

respectively. The judge wrote as follows:

> Defendants, acting individually and jointly, and in conspira-
> cy with each other, intentionally interfered with plaintiff's
> contractual rights and economic relations, and did so *will-*
> *fully, with malice, without justification, and with wanton dis-*
> *regard for the law and the rights of others.* In consequence,
> the circumstances of this case warrant the imposition of sub-
> stantial punitive damages against [Arthur and Bill Wirtz].[22]
> (Emphasis added).

....

WHO WANTS TO BE A MONOPOLIST?

The Wirtzes know a little secret that the rest of us don't: you can become
very rich in the free market, but in order to become rich as Rockefeller, you
have to have a monopoly. The creation, maintenance, and abuse of their
monopoly power has been the keystone of the Wirtz family's business tactics
for years. Bill Wirtz and his family are among the most persistent and egregious violators of the antitrust laws in *all* of American history. They have
been involved in major antitrust litigation in the 1950s, 1970s, 1980s, and
1990s. (They're the Minnie Minosa of antitrust violators.)

In addition to the two antitrust cases discussed already, a third major case
involved the NHL's antitrust violations against the World Hockey
Association, in which Bill Wirtz played a major part.[23] In that case, the court
found that the NHL conspired to monopolize major league professional hockey by controlling the pool of available players and expanding the NHL so as
to thwart the WHA. Similarly, in 1972, the Blackhawks also distinguished
themselves from their business peers by becoming one of the few companies
to be convicted for violating the Federal Wage and Price Control Act, for
instituting a 50 percent hockey program price increase in 1971.

Yet another antitrust case occurred in 1992 when Blueline Publishing,
Inc. sued the Blackhawks for denying its hockey program media credentials,
which harmed *The Blue Line's* ability to compete against the Blackhawks in
the market for day-of-the-game programs.[24] Likewise, in 1995, a group of 17

---

[22]*Fishman v. Estate of Wirtz et al.*, 594 F. Supp. 853 at 887.

[23]See *Philadelphia World Hockey Club, Inc. v. National Hockey League, et al.* 351 F.
Supp. 462 (1972).

[24]See Introduction herein, pp. v-vii. See also *Mark G. Weinberg and Blue Line Publishing,
Inc. v. Chicago Blackhawk Hockey Team, Inc.*, 653 N.E.2d 1322, 210 Ill.Dec. 860 (1995).

independent peanut vendors sued Bill Wirtz and the other owners of the United Center on antitrust grounds for being the first sports stadium in the country to ban patrons from bringing peanuts inside, a blatant effort to monopolize food concession sales at the United Center.[25]

Indeed, most of the Wirtz family's business tactics can be viewed in the light of efforts to obtain and exploit their monopoly power. Even Bill Wirtz's well-known opposition to the expansion of the NHL from six to 12 teams in the 1960s can be seen as a means to retain monopoly power. Desirous of maintaining their exclusive control over hockey, Norris and Wirtz were able to stifle expansion for years, even while the other major sports expanded and thrived.[26] It was not until 1966 that the league finally expand from their original six teams. Perhaps in this time of ill-conceived overexpansion to every hamlet in the country, it's possible to look back wistfully at Wirtz's reluctance to expand the NHL. But his reluctance to expand did not stem from any concern for the welfare or integrity of the sport but from naked self-interest. In a smaller league, Wirtz and Norris ran the show without challenge, and while expansion would make the sport of hockey more accessible and popular to the masses, it would also reduce Wirtz and Norris' monopoly control.

The family's defenders argue that the Wirtzes' status as one of the country's preeminent violators of the antitrust laws is the result of vigorous and aggressive business practices, which should be applauded, not condemned. Moreover, they argue that the family's pattern of antitrust violations over several decades is the result of ambiguities in the antitrust law itself. While it's true that ambiguities exist in the law and that there is sometimes a fine line between respectability and rapacity, it's equally true that it is quite difficult to violate the antitrust laws as often as the Wirtz family has. To do so, you have to work damn hard at it. The antitrust laws are interpreted so one-sidedly in favor of big business one has to play *exceedingly* dirty to be found guilty. Neither federal nor state governments bring antitrust cases easily and, given the expense and difficulty of proving a case, third parties are extremely reluctant to bring cases. Virtually the only way to be found in violation of the

---

[25]See *Elliot v. United Center*, 126 F.3d 1003 (1997 7th Cir); 523 U.S. 1021; 118 S. Ct. 1998 (cert. denied). There are other examples of Wirtz's grab for monopoly power. In 1999, Bill Wirtz used his access to public officials to purchase a state-sanctioned monopoly in liquor distribution in the state of Illinois by having special-interest legislation passed on his behalf. Over the years, Wirtz also has used his contacts with City of Chicago officials to obtain monopolies on concession sales for the Wirtz-owned Bismarck foods at the Chicago Park District and at Navy Pier. See chapter five herein, pp. 55-69.

[26]As hockey writer Stan Fischler has documented, Bill Wirtz and James Norris, Jr. refused every effort to expand the NHL for as long as they could. See Stan Fischler, *Slashing!*, Thomas Y. Crowell Company, New York, 1974, p. 68.

antitrust laws as often as the Wirtz family has is to arrogantly ignore the law or willingly and repeatedly push the law to its breaking point.

But then who can blame the Wirtzes for their arrogance? The reality is that in our society there is little price to be paid for violating the antitrust laws. Monopolists like the Wirtzes are accorded a forgiveness for their crimes that encourages them to continue breaking the law. Economics 101 teaches us that the reaping of illegal monopoly profits is pure stealing, but it is a sophisticated, high-end form of stealing that tends not to outrage the public in comparison to the crimes of others. There are several reasons for this. A monopolist's crimes are not committed against any one individual but against consumers at large. Such diffuse harms tend not to generate outrage like a single, concrete murder or theft. In addition, any check on the abuse of private economic rights smells like Bolshevism to many Americans. And monopolists seem to be the beneficiary of a sort of Darwinian double-standard, whereby those of the lower class who break the law are criminals, but those of the upper class who break the law are proof of some superiority and rightful dominance. In America, the monopolist is our society's "winner." If the monopolist wasn't superior in some way, he wouldn't have his monopoly, or so the thinking goes.

"My only crime was loving her too much...
well, that and stealing from her trust fund."

CHAPTER 3

Stealing from His "Niece's" Trust Fund

"If Heaven had looked upon riches to be such a valuable thing, it would not have given them to such a scoundrel."

— *Jonathan Swift*

In December 1985, a Chicago jury needed less than three hours of deliberation to find that Bill Wirtz had cheated Susan Norris out of the proper value of her trust fund when she was 18 years old. The jury found that Wirtz illegally sold stock from Susan's trust fund at bargain basement prices and that the sale benefitted the Wirtz family's own corporate interests. Norris was awarded damages of $1.54 million plus interest. This revolting episode revealed Bill Wirtz's willingness to exploit even the most vulnerable of victims, as well as a willingness to betray the trust of those closest to him. It's one thing to rip-off customers you don't know or take advantage of business rivals who are presumably in a position to protect themselves, but preying on the weak and defenseless who have placed their trust in you is completely indefensible. For sheer rottenness, this incident qualifies as the lowest of Wirtz's crimes.[1]

Susan Norris was born in 1949. She was the only child of James D. Norris, Jr. The Wirtz and Norris families were the closest of business associates. Almost all of the Norris and Wirtz business interests were jointly owned, including sports teams, real estate, banking and liquor. The Norris-Wirtz con-

---

[1] I have summarized the facts of the case in this chapter, but interested readers can find the full opinions at *Norris v. Wirtz*, 551 F. Supp. 46 (1982); *Norris v. Wirtz*, 1983 U.S. App. Lexis 14248 (December 22, 1983); *Norris v. Wirtz*, 719 F.2d 256 (7th Cir. 1983); and *Norris v. Wirtz*, 818 F.2d 1329 (7th Cir. 1987), cert. denied, 484 U.S. 943, 108 S. Ct. 329, 98 L. Ed. 2d 356 (1987).

nection began in 1933, when Arthur Wirtz and James Norris, Sr., Susan Norris' grandfather, teamed up to buy Olympia Stadium in Detroit and the Detroit Red Wings. After James Norris, Sr. died in 1952, James Norris, Jr. took over the family's business with the Wirtzes.

In February 1966, Susan's father, Jim Norris, Jr., died at age 59. Prior to his death, he had named his wife, Mary, and his life-long business associate, Bill Wirtz, as co-executors of his estate. Norris' will gave certain personal property to his wife, then divided any remaining property into two trusts, one for the benefit of his wife, Mary, and the other for the benefit of his daughter, Susan. Susan's trust was to pay her a regular income until she reached the age of 40. Then at 40, she was entitled to withdraw half the principal, and at age 50 she was entitled to withdraw the remaining principal.

The will appointed Bill Wirtz as trustee of both trusts. When Norris, Jr. died, the assets in his estate consisted in large part of assets which he had owned with the Wirtzes. These included Chicago Stadium Corporation (which owned and operated the Chicago Stadium), the St. Louis Arena Corporation (the largest sports stadium in St. Louis at the time), Judge & Dolph, Ltd. (a liquor wholesaler), Consolidated Enterprises, Inc. (which owned the Chicago Blackhawks Hockey Team, a liquor business, and certain real estate interests), and shares of stock of Spring Hills Farms, Inc. (a stable of races horses). In designating Bill Wirtz as the co-executor of his estate and the trustee of his wife and daughter's trust funds, Jim Norris had placed his trust and confidence in Bill Wirtz.

As Jim Norris' only child, Susan had known Arthur and Bill Wirtz all her life. Bill was nineteen years older than Susan and not just a close family friend but also "a surrogate father."[2] She trusted Bill Wirtz and regarded herself as Bill's "niece." At trial, she explained that she didn't feel the need to protect herself from any self-dealing from the Wirtzes with regard to her trust fund, saying, "I trusted Bill Wirtz and Arthur Wirtz...completely."[3] Neither Susan Norris nor her mother, Mary, had any knowledge of the mutual business activities of the Wirtzes and Norrises.[4] Susan Norris testified that she had never even heard of the three corporations in which her interests were sold by and to her "trusted" friend and fiduciary, Bill Wirtz. She had a high

[2]818 F.2d at 1337 (dissent).

[3]Trial transcript, Case No. 80 C 6836 at 1446.

[4]As the appellate court put it, "The Wirtzes, in line with their usual view of a women's place, excluded Susan and her mother from any role in the businesses of which they were joint owners." 818 F.2d 1337 (dissent). Arthur and Bill Wirtz are known to look askance at women in business. Bill Wirtz' ex-brother-in-law, Mr. John Roney, told the author in personal conversation on June 12, 2000 that none of the Wirtz family women are even permitted to be involved in the family businesses.

school education, no business experience, no personal attorney, no investment advisor and no stockbroker. Nobody was watching out for her interests, except good ol' Uncle Bill. Similarly, Susan's mother, Mary, had no business experience, had not gone to college or business or accounting school. And she too trusted the Wirtzes. In everyday conversation, Mary Norris called Arthur Wirtz, "Uncle Arthur."

In contrast, Arthur and Bill Wirtz had intimate knowledge of all of their businesses. They were actively engaged in running all of them. As the plaintiff's lawyers put it in closing arguments at Susan Norris' trial, "If ever there was an unequal match when it came to the transactions in this case — a gross mismatch — it was between Arthur and Bill Wirtz on the one hand, and Mary and Susan Norris on the other. One side, with Bill Wirtz in a fiduciary capacity, having knowledge of all the facts concerning the business, and the other side with none of them."[5]

LIFE'S A BREACH

In 1967 and 1968, in breach of his fiduciary duties, Bill Wirtz sold stock in Susan Norris' trust at reduced prices to benefit his own family. Rather than selling her assets at fair market value, Wirtz sold the assets in Norris' trust at book value to corporations that the Wirtz family already controlled.[6] In the process, Wirtz deceived Susan Norris into believing she was getting fair market value for her assets. As Susan Norris' trustee, Bill Wirtz was obligated to get the best possible price for her, yet he knowingly concealed the true value of the assets. As the purchaser of Susan's assets, the Wirtz family ended up being a bigger beneficiary of Susan Norris' assets than even Susan Norris. As the court in this case observed, when Bill Wirtz's self-dealing was over, "the Wirtzes effectively controlled all three of the closely-held corporations in which the estate held stocks, and to that extent became more of a beneficiary under the will than did plaintiff, the decedent's daughter."[7] In short, Bill Wirtz, in an egregious act of self-dealing, cheated and defrauded his "niece" for the sole purpose of benefiting his own family's financial interests.

The particulars of Wirtz's fleecing of Susan involve the sale of stock in three separate corporations: St. Louis Arena Corp., which controlled St. Louis stadium; Arena Bowl Inc., a bowling alley next to the St. Louis stadium; and Judge & Dolph Ltd., a Chicago wholesale liquor outlet. The stock of St. Louis Arena Corp. and Arena Bowl, Inc. were sold at grossly unfair

[5]Trial transcript, Case No. 80 C 6836 at 1975.

[6]In most of the corporations in Susan's trust, the Wirtzes owned 51 percent of the stock and James Norris owned 49 percent.

[7]719 F.2d at 258.

prices, and Wirtz knew, or would have known had he not acted recklessly, that the fair market value of the stock was substantially greater than the price he paid for it and that Susan Norris had no clue as to its true value.

The Sale of Stock of the St. Louis Arena: On September 21, 1967, Bill Wirtz, on behalf of the Norris estate, sold 4,993 shares (49.93 percent) of stock of St. Louis Arena Corporation. The St. Louis Arena was the largest indoor sports facility in St. Louis and would be the future home of the St. Louis Blues upon their entrance into the NHL in 1967. Bill Wirtz procured Susan Norris' written but uninformed consent to the transaction. Wirtz, however, did not tell Susan that upon being sold, the Wirtz family would own 100 percent of the St. Louis Arena. In addition, he did not disclose that the $2,600,000 purchase price for the shares was grossly inadequate. Wirtz based the purchase price on the corporation's last available balance sheet, dated June 30, 1967. But as the court found, presenting the balance sheet as the basis for the sale price was completely invalid because it only represented the *book value* of the corporation and not its *fair market* value.

Wirtz's attorneys argued that book value was a fair valuation of assets for a minority shareholder in a closely-held corporation.[8] But no one bought the argument. Book value is simply the cost of goods, minus depreciation, subtracted by liabilities. It has absolutely no relation to fair market value. Book value refers to the cost of the original purchase price of an asset. In the case of the St. Louis Arena, the figures Wirtz used to determine the price he paid Susan for her stock was based on the cost of the land, building and equipment in the 1940s, decades before the transaction in question. At trial, it was shown that the value of the land had a balance sheet (a.k.a. book) value of $117,650.58 or 11 cents a square foot. But the fair market value of the land, based on recent sales and expert testimony, was $1.50 a square foot, almost 15 times more than the Wirtzes' paid Susan for it. A year and a half after buying the assets from Susan for just 11 cents a square foot, the Wirtzes sold the land for $1.50 a square foot to the new owners of the St. Louis Blues.[9]

---

[8]Wirtz himself testified that the book value was a fair price. "I considered it a fair price for those shares," he asserted. Trial transcript, Case No. 80 C 6836, p. 393.

[9]At trial, Norris' lawyers mocked and disparaged Wirtz's contention that Susan received fair value for the assets. If the price was fair, they asked the jury, "would we not have heard somebody come in, an expert? Would there not have been Wirtz experts on that stand, would there not have been a real estate appraiser from St. Louis to contradict Mr. McReynolds' figures of a dollar fifty, fifteen times what Susan Norris was paid for that real estate? Would there not have been somebody to get on the stand to testify that the stock was worth — was fairly priced in this transaction? Nobody appeared." *Id.* at 1987.

Bill Wirtz testified under oath that he never actually bothered to have anyone do a real valuation of the assets of the St. Louis Arena:

> *Lawyer:* Peat, Marwick did not perform any appraisal of the fair market value of the shares, did they?
> *Wirtz:* We conferred with Peat, Marwick as far as...
> *Lawyer:* Mr. Wirtz, did you ask them to appraise the fair market value of the shares?
> *Objection By Wirtz's Lawyer:* Your Honor, I am going to object to the interruption of the answer.
> *Judge:* Really, I have asked him to interrupt him when he sees the answer is veering off. It's a 'yes' or 'no' answer. He is entitled to a 'yes' or 'no' answer. Could you please answer it 'yes' or 'no?'
> *Wirtz:* No.[10]

Indeed, the only valuation of the property done was by Arthur and Bill Wirtz in their own heads for their own personal financial gain. The testimony revealed that there were no serious negotiations over the value of the property. Though Bill Wirtz as trustee was required by law to get the best possible price he could for the St. Louis Arena, all he seemingly did was sit down with his father, ask him what he was willing to pay for it, and sold it to him at that price. As Susan Norris' lawyer put it at closing arguments: "In 1967, we submit, ladies and gentleman, Arthur Wirtz decided to take the property of St. Louis and to get it as cheap as he could. He sat down with Bill and said, 'I'll buy it at book.' And Bill Wirtz agreed. 'I'll sell it to you at book.'"[11]

The Sale of Stock of Arena Bowl: The Arena Bowl was a 72-lane bowling alley in St. Louis. The circumstances surrounding the sale of the Arena Bowl corresponded exactly with the sale of the St. Louis Arena. On September 21, 1967, the same date on which the stock in the St. Louis Arena Corp. was sold, Bill Wirtz sold 8,625 shares (50 percent) of stock of Arena Bowl, Inc. Bill Wirtz purchased the shares from Susan's trust for $86,265. Again, Wirtz got Susan's written but uninformed consent to the transaction. Again, he failed to inform Susan that the purchase price of $86,265 was grossly inadequate since it was based on book value and in no way reflected the fair market value of the assets. Again, he failed to inform the Norrises that Wirtz Corp. was the only other shareholder. Again, no other evidence of the stock's value was submitted by Wirtz to Mary Norris, Susan Norris, or the

---

[10]Trial transcript, Case No. 80 C 6836 at 221.
[11]*Id.* at 1978.

Probate court. Again, Wirtz testified at trial that he didn't bother to have anybody actually do a real valuation of the assets. And again, the only valuation of the property done was by Arthur and Bill Wirtz in their own heads for their own purposes.

The Sale of Stock of Judge & Dolph. Ltd: Approximately one year after the sale of stock in the St. Louis Arena and Arena Bowl, on September 27, 1968, Bill Wirtz, on behalf of the Norris estate, sold 8,625 shares (5.75 percent) of stock from Susan's trust of Judge and Dolph. Ltd. at $20.00 a share for a total price of $172,500. This time, Bill Wirtz really sold his "niece" down the river. The Wirtz family owned 75 percent of the stock; the Norris estate owned 5.75 percent; and two other dissenting investors owned a combined 19.25 percent. Again, the amount paid to the estate was grossly inadequate. As before, the sale of the shares was based on the company's book value, not fair market value. But this time there was an additional factor that made the assets in Susan Norris' trust especially valuable and for which she received no compensation whatsoever from the manipulating Wirtz.

Arthur Wirtz was desperate to obtain the 5.75 percent of the Norris estates' shares in order to accomplish his objective of obtaining full ownership of Judge & Dolph. By obtaining the stock owned by Norris, Arthur Wirtz would control over 80 percent of the outstanding stock. Under the law, this would allow him to force a dissolution of the company and a redemption of the outstanding shares of the other two minority investors, thus making Judge & Dolph a wholly-owned subsidiary of Wirtz Corp. The two minority investors, the ice skating legend Sonje Henie and a businessman named Victor Brust, refused to sell their interests to Wirtz for the paltry $20.00 a share he was offering. Accordingly, Susan was sitting in precisely the type of situation in which a substantial premium could be expected to be paid a minority shareholder for the shares. Yet no such premium was paid. Instead, Susan's shares were sold to the Wirtzes for the measly $20.00 a share, which turned out to be substantially less than either Sonje Heine or Victor Brust eventually received. In 1969, less than a year after the Wirtzes had bought Susan's shares for $20.00 each, Arthur Wirtz paid $28.00 per share to the estate of Sonje Heine for her shares and $33.00 in stock in a separate Wirtz-owned entity to Victor Brust for his shares.

Besides cheating Susan out of the fair market value for her holdings in Judge & Dolph, the trial also revealed that Wirtz never even bothered to get Susan's approval for the sale of her Judge & Dolph shares. Whereas in the two other stock sales, Wirtz actually went about getting Susan's written but uninformed consent, here Bill never even sought Susan's permission. Under the terms of James Norris' will, Susan's approval of all sales involving the Wirtzes and the estate's assets was required.[12] In his defense, Wirtz admitted that, while he never discussed the transaction with Susan, he had assumed that Susan's mother, Mary, had explained everything to her and had obtained her approval of it.[13] But even if Mary had discussed the facts of the sale with her daughter, which her daughter denied and which could not be shown because Mary died in 1976 well before this 1985 trial, Wirtz's own statement on its face amounts to an admission that he violated his fiduciary duties. A fundamental principle of trust law is that a trustee is required to fully disclose *to the beneficiary* all facts upon which the beneficiary must exercise judgment.[14]

Wirtz's cunning did not end with selling out Susan's interests at below-market prices or with failing to get her informed (or even uninformed) consent to the transactions. Evidence at trail revealed that Wirtz's final deceit involved falsely representing to both Mary Norris and the Probate court that Judge & Dolph was "to be liquidated and dissolved." This was a bald-faced lie. Wirtz knew that Judge & Dolph was not going to be liquidated and dissolved. Indeed, it is still owned and operated by the Wirtz family to this day and is one of the largest wholesale liquor companies in the country.

In claiming Judge & Dolph was "to be liquidated and dissolved," Wirtz was playing fast and loose with the truth to give the Probate Court and Mary Norris the impression that the sale of Judge & Dolph's stock from Susan's trust was part of a plan by the Wirtzes to get out of the liquor business. In fact, the Wirtzes' intent was the exact opposite: their goal was to consolidate their control over Judge & Dolph. True, the company was dissolved two years after the Norris estates' sale of its Judge & Dolph shares to the Wirtzes, but the company had no intention of going out of business. It simply went through some corporate maneuvering so that Judge & Dolph could become a wholly-owned subsidiary operation under the Wirtz family's corporate umbrella.

ONE HAND ON THE BIBLE; THE OTHER WITH FINGERS CROSSED

During this trial, Wirtz was once again ridiculed for his courtroom deceit and slippery tactics. At most trials, a witness' deposition testimony is rarely

---

[12]719 F.2d 256 at 261.

[13]Plaintiff's attorney: "You personally had no discussion with Susan Norris concerning the Judge & Dolph transaction. That is correct, is it not?" Wirtz: "That is correct." Trial transcript, Case No. 80 C 6836 at 392.

[14]Restatement (Second) of Trusts sec. 173, Comment d (1959).

used against him unless he has contradicted himself on the stand. In this case, however, Susan's lawyers consistently read Wirtz's prior testimony to make it clear to everyone that Wirtz had changed his story from the deposition to the trial. For example, in his deposition testimony, Wirtz claimed he never spoke to Susan about these transactions, but then at trial he claimed the exact opposite, saying his recollection was now refreshed and that he had had long conversations with Susan and had shown her all sorts of documents related to these transactions.[15] In the closing arguments, Susan Norris' lawyers emphasized Wirtz's lack of credibility to the jury: "Where a witness testifies one way at a deposition and testifies another way here in the courtroom, you will decide which version is the truth. Mr. Wirtz did this repeatedly."[16]

SAVED BY THE STATUTE OF LIMITATIONS

Though the jury found Wirtz guilty of breaching his fiduciary duty to Susan Norris, in 1987 an appellate court nullified the jury's decision. In a two-to-one ruling, the appellate court agreed with Wirtz's attorneys that, under Illinois law, Susan's initial filing of the lawsuit on Dec. 24, 1980, over 12 years after the transactions had occurred, missed the three-year statute of limitations for securities fraud actions.[17] Wirtz's lawyers argued that Susan knew full well of Wirtz's shady dealings long before she actually filed the lawsuit. Norris' lawyers countered that she was too young and naive during the crucial period to know that she had been duped. The appellate court found that Susan was entitled to postpone the running of the statute for several years, but that since 1975 Susan had been dealing with Bill at arm's length through independent attorneys and that certainly by November 1977, over three years prior to when the suit was actually filed, Susan knew enough to recognize that she had been a victim of fraud.

The appellate court's decision was hardly vindication for Wirtz. The court did not question any of the facts surrounding the fraud[18] and acknowledged that Wirtz's actions constituted a serious "conflict of interest" and

---

[15]Trial transcript, Case No. 80 C 6836 at 1986.

[16]Trial transcript, Case No. 80 C 6836 at 1972-3.

[17]See 818 F.2d 1329 (7th Cir. 1987). Judge Richard Cudahy dissented from the court's majority opinion, arguing that Norris was simply too young and naive at the time of the stock transactions in the late 1960s for the statute of limitations to be applicable: "When an adolescent girl is allegedly defrauded by her trustee, who is also an old family friend and essentially a surrogate father, under circumstances like these, I see little reason to distrust the jury verdict." *Id.* at 1340 (dissent).

[18]*Id.* at 1334. ("The facts are largely undisputed," wrote the court. *Id.*)

called what Wirtz did "deceit."[19] Nevertheless, the court held that the lawsuit was "untimely"[20] and overturned the jury's verdict on that basis.[21]

Susan lost the case, but not the battle. On February 17, 1984, Susan brought a second lawsuit against Wirtz for sabotaging her trust fund in transactions that occurred within the statute of limitations. In particular, she filed a lawsuit alleging that Wirtz had deprived her of his honest and faithful performance of his duties as trustee of her estate in a series of transactions that were made in 1975, 1979, 1981, 1982, 1983, and 1984. This time, Wirtz chose not to fight Susan in court, opting instead to settle out of court for an undisclosed amount of money and an undisclosed amount of shame.

[19]*Id.* at 1331,1334.
[20]*Id.* at 1335, 1336.
[21]*Id.* at 1334.

"Let us prey."

CHAPTER 4

Bribing Public Officials

"If you can't be good, at least be careful."

— *Mark Twain*

Through an anonymous source inside the United Center, I have obtained evidence that shows Bill Wirtz and Jerry Reinsdorf bribed a Chicago alderman in exchange for the alderman's support of legislation to ban all outside vending at the United Center. This is the first time this information has been made public. There's an old saying among Chicago politicians: "Never write when you can speak. Never speak when you can nod. And never nod when you can wink." Given the existence of a paper trail confirming this bribe, such wisdom of the ages was apparently forgotten here.

In October of 1995, the City Counsel of Chicago passed an ordinance that banned all peddling in a radius of 1,000 feet of the United Center. The new section 4-244-147 of the Chicago Municipal Code now reads as follows: "No person shall peddle merchandise of any type on any portion of the public way within 1,000 feet of the United Center." The legislation was purportedly passed for crowd control purposes, but as the facts reveal, the legislation was actually passed solely to benefit the financial interests of Bill Wirtz and Jerry Reinsdorf. The effect of the ordinance was to grant Wirtz and Reinsdorf a monopoly on all food and merchandise concession sales at the United Center.

Prior to passage of the ordinance in 1995, it was common for peanut, hat, t-shirt, and other merchandise vendors to sell their wares on the public sidewalks outside Bulls and Blackhawks games at the old Chicago Stadium. These vendors competed in a fair manner with the food and merchandise sold inside the stadium. The goods of the outside vendors were almost always less expensive. As one patron put it, "Only a fool would buy peanuts inside the stadium." The 1995 ordinance, however, prohibited the vendors from working within 1,000-foot radius of the stadium, putting them well beyond the normal foot traffic at games. This effectively destroyed the vendors' businesses. As a result, other than program vendors who are protected by the First Amendment, there are now no longer any vendors outside the United Center.

LET'S MAKE A DEAL

Two documents in my possession, written by a high-level United Center executive, show that the operators of the United Center were involved in a secret and illegal deal with Chicago Alderman Dexter Watson of the 27th ward and Illinois State Senator Rickey Hendon to arrange passage of an ordinance banning street vending within 1,000 feet of the United Center. (The 27th ward encompasses the United Center.) The documents clearly show that in exchange for the alderman and senator's sponsorship and support of the ordinance, Wirtz and Reinsdorf were willing to hire four employees of Watson and Hendon's choosing to be employed by Bismarck Food Service, the Wirtz-owned concession company inside the United Center.

It may strike some readers that Wirtz and Reinsdorf's offer to a couple of local politicians to control four concessionaire jobs inside the United Center is small potatoes, but it just goes to show that the current market rate for purchasing such self-serving municipal legislation isn't really all that high. Moreover, though the offer to Watson and Hendon to control four jobs inside the United Center was not a bribe in the time-honored manner of offering cash under the table, it nonetheless constituted a blatant attempt at bribery by offering valuable patronage opportunities to Watson and Hendon so they could then reward their own political supporters with jobs, which itself is a well-respected, time-honored Chicago tradition.

The first document, dated July 26, 1994, is an internal memorandum by Howard Pizer, who was then the project manager of the United Center and is now the executive vice president of the United Center. It was written to his immediate superiors, Bill Wirtz and Jerry Reinsdorf. (See Exhibit A, pages 40-41.) The other document is a letter, dated August 25, 1994, from Mr. Pizer to a Mr. John Reyes of the office of the 27th ward. This letter is carbon copied to both Wirtz and Reinsdorf. (See Exhibit B, pages 42-43.) Both documents spell out the terms of a deal between the operators of the United Center and Alderman Watson and Senator Hendon to pass a 1,000-foot ordinance banning all peddling on the public property outside the United Center in exchange for Watson and Hendon's control over certain United Center jobs.

In its particulars, the *quid pro quo* here involved the United Center's agreeing to "make available to Rickey and Dexter two program stands in the United Center." By "make available," Pizer means ceding control of the hiring of these particular program vendors to Watson and Hendon. This is made abundantly clear in the memorandum when Pizer writes, "[t]he people to be operating these stands will be selected by Rickey and Dexter." In exchange for ceding control of the "program stands," the United Center expects Watson to support the United Center's efforts to ban peddling within a 1,000-foot radius of the arena. In the memorandum, Pizer writes:

> It would be made clear that the Joint Venture [a reference to the United Center] is only agreeing to this reluctantly and would not do so unless it resolved existing problems and disagreements with Senator Hendon and Alderman Watson. Therefore, *it is expected that we will receive the cooperation of these parties so far as the Horner Annex, the West Damen Parking, and the 1,000 foot ordinance are concerned.* (Emphasis added.)

In Pizer's letter to John Reyes, dated August 25, 1994, Pizer specifies the number of vendors to be involved in the arrangement and defines the positions to be afforded the new employees: one would be "placed in a program stand position in the United Center;" one "would be placed in a novelty selling position in the United Center;" and two others would be placed in "novelty seller positions on our property outside the building."

As it turned out, this particular deal was never actually pulled off by the parties involved, for prior to the passage of the ordinance Dexter Watson lost his reelection bid to current alderman, Walter Burnett. It was ultimately Burnett who sponsored the 1,000-foot ordinance in October of 1995. There is no reason to think that Burnett was bribed for his support of the legislation. As a matter of fact, despite his initial support for the legislation in 1995, Ald. Burnett has subsequently made it clear that he regrets supporting the anti-peddling legislation and that Wirtz and Reinsdorf lied to him about its purpose.

Coming full circle, Ald. Burnett has acknowledged that the purpose behind the ban on peddling outside the United Center was nothing but a ploy by Wirtz and Reinsdorf to monopolize the vending business at the United Center: "They [United Center officials] tried to make it look like it wasn't just greed — they said they didn't want peddlers harassing people, trying to make sales. *But it was clear from the beginning that what they really wanted was the peddlers' business.*" (Emphasis added.) And concerning Ald. Burnett's support of the legislation, Ald. Burnett added, "I've never been

EXHIBIT A

Copy of July 26, 1994 Internal Memorandum
Establishing Terms of Illegal *Quid Pro Quo*

DRAFT

TO: Bill Wirtz, Jerry Reinsdorf
FROM: Howard Pizer
DATE: July 26, 1994
RE: Positions at the United Center

The purpose of this memo is to set forth our proposal to Senator Hendon and Alderman Watson. It is important that we agree with the premises underlying this proposal, because if it is accepted we should all know what commitments we have made. The proposal is as follows:

1. We would make available to Rickey and Dexter two program stands in the United Center. The arrangement will be set up on an entrepreneurial basis whereby the United Center (or Bismarck) would sell the programs to the operator of the stand who would then resell the programs to our patrons at the stated price. The pricing would be structured so that the profit would be the same (20%) as the existing union members who operate the stands as Bismarck employees.

2. The people to be operating these stands will be selected by Rickey and Dexter, but would be subject to all the same rules and regulations that all people actually employed by Bismarck are subject. This would include grooming standards, drug testing, courtesy training, etc.

3. If at any time the operator should violate these rules, he or 'she would be subject to termination.

4. The individuals operating the stands would be required to join the union.

5. As we have already used up any goodwill that we might have with the union, it would be up to Rickey to work out an arrangement with the union to obtain these stands since these two stands will be taken away from existing union people to be given to the community.

6. The operators will be required to obtain all necessary business, tax and other licenses associated with entrepreneurship as opposed to employment status.

7. This arrangement would continue on an indefinite basis so long as the circumstances giving rise to this understanding continue to exist.

EXHIBIT A (cont.)

July 26, 1994
Page Two

8.   It would be made clear that the Joint Venture is only agreeing to this reluctantly and would not do so unless it resolved existing problems and disagreements with Senator Hendon and Alderman Watson. Therefore, it is expected that we will receive the cooperation of these parties so far as the Horner Annex, the West of Damen Parking, and the 1,000 foot ordinance are concerned.

9.   It is also assumed that no other requests will be made by the Alderman and Senator.

HCP/lap

EXHIBIT B
Copy of August 25, 1994 Letter
Codifying Terms of Illegal *Quid Pro Quo*

⩊ UNITED CENTER

YER · EYES – only
cc. D. WATSON
SEN. HENDON
8-26-95

August 25, 1994

Mr. John Reyes
c/o 27th Ward Office
538 N. Western Avenue
Chicago, IL 60612

Dear John,

The purpose of this letter is to set forth the following understanding which we tentatively reached at our meeting on Friday, August 19:

1. Four community residents, some of whom may have experience in the food service business, would be hired by Bismarck Enterprises to implement a "mentor/protege" program. Obviously these individuals would be subject to normal Bismarck hiring standards and procedures. They would then work in various positions at the United Center with the goal that they enhance their existing skills through participation in various aspects of the United Center food service operations. As we have discussed, you would be responsible to resolve any union problems raised by this program. Our goal would be that these individuals, after a period of time, which I would expect to vary from person to person, would be in a position to have sufficient entrepreneurial skills to manage a concession stand. This is subject to possible union problems which you will be expected to resolve.

2. One community resident would be placed in a program stand position in the United Center for Bulls and Blackhawks games. The person selected for this position would become a normal Bismarck employee, and would be subject to normal Bismarck hiring standards and procedures. This is subject to possible union problems which you will be expected to resolve.

3. One community resident would be placed in a novelty selling position in the United Center for Bulls and Blackhawks games. The person selected for this position would become a normal Bismarck employee, and would be subject to normal Bismarck hiring standards and procedures. This is subject to possible union problems which you will be expected to resolve.

333 West 35th Street Chicago IL 60616
312·451·5501 Fax: 312·451·5519

EXHIBIT B (cont.)

Mr. John Reyes
August 25, 1994
Page 2

4. As we have previously discussed, we will provide the community with more than half of the outside novelty seller positions on our property outside of the building. Initially there may only be two positions, but we would expect this to increase over time. We would provide inventory and other necessities for operations. Again, these individuals would be subject to normal Bismarck hiring standards and procedures. These vendors would receive 10% of net sales (after deducting sales tax) of the merchandise sold by them at Bulls and Blackhawks games. The percentage would be 8% for most other events.

5. As we also discussed, the United Center Joint Venture is willing and anxious to assist in financing economic development in the community. Toward this end, we have committed a $200,000 economic development fund. Obviously before any investment would be made by us, we would have to be certain of the anticipated community benefit as well as be comfortable that the proposed business has a realistic chance of success.

It is our understanding that if the above program is implemented, this will address all of Senator Hendon's and Alderman Watson's concerns.

Very truly yours,

Howard Pizer

Howard C. Pizer
Executive Vice President

HCP/lap
cc: Bill Wirtz
       Jerry Reinsdorf

pushed so hard on anything in my life."[1]

Even ignoring Ald. Burnett's astonishing admission, the two documents offered here by themselves reveal an undeniable intent by the United Center to engage in an illegal bribe to purchase special legislation. Unquestionably, Wirtz and Reinsdorf's defenders will argue that, technically speaking, there was no actual bribe here because, in the end, Ald. Watson never took part in the legislation's passage and the control of the four jobs at Bismarck Foods were never actually given to the politicians. But a technical legal defense, while perhaps effective in court, makes no difference in revealing Wirtz and Reinsdorf's underhanded business practices and corrupt tactics. Indeed, a technical legal defense isn't an excuse for the actions at all— it is, rather, part of the problem. In our society, it seems that proving a crime has become virtually the only test for unacceptable behavior, and anything that can't be proven for absolute certainty to a judge or jury becomes acceptable. But it is a flawed premise to assume the only way to judge whether someone has engaged in wrongdoing, even criminal wrongdoing, is for the allegations to be proved in a court of law. Not only does such a standard benefit the rich, who have the legal resources to hire the cleverest and most experienced lawyers and who are thus least likely to be found guilty under any circumstances in a court of law, but it reinforces the faulty idea that legal definitions alone should be the measure of a man's scruples.[2]

IT AIN'T JUST PEANUTS, FOLKS!

In ridding themselves of the peanut vendors, Wirtz and Reinsdorf easily stand to gain hundreds of thousand — perhaps millions — of dollars a year. Do the math: Conservatively, there were 20 peanut vendors selling outside any Blackhawks or Bulls game. An average bag of peanuts cost $2.00; each vendor sold on average 75 bags per game. Thus, there were approximately 1500 bags of peanuts sold per game for a take of $3,000 ($2.00 x 1500 = $3,000). If just half the patrons who used to buy a bag of peanuts on the outside now spend $6.00 on the inside to satisfy their junk food craving, that's

---

[1]John Carpenter and Charles Nicodemus, "How City Hall Banned Vendors Near Arenas," *Chicago Sun-Times*, January 11, 1998, p. 1.

[2]Oliver Wendel Holmes said the definition of a man of dubious character is one whose only moral restraint is the law. "If you want to know the law and nothing else, you must look at it as a bad man, who cares only for the material consequences which such knowledge enables him to predict, not as a good one, who finds his reasons for conduct, whether inside the law or outside of it, in the vaguer sanctions of conscience." Oliver Wendell Holmes, *The Path of the Law*, in *The Mind and Faith of Justice Holmes* 74 (Max Lerner ed., 1989).

$4,500 a game in increased revenue for the United Center ($6.00 x 750 = $4,500). Multiply that by a minimum of 90 Blackhawks and Bulls games a year, plus 110 dates for concerts, circus, and ice shows, and it comes to $900,000 in additional gross revenue per year ($4,500 x 200 = $900,000). And that's just the peanut concession business. This estimate doesn't even factor in the money gained by Wirtz and Reinsdorf by having eliminated through their backroom dealings the ability of t-shirt and hat vendors to ply their trades outside the United Center.

Bill Wirtz: A Life In Pictures*

Born Nov. 5, 1930, Bill Wirtz is seen here playing with his first toy, the Playskool Skybox Profit Fun Pot Set.© Regarding his humble beginnings in the midst of the Great Depression, Wirtz recalls, "It was tough growing up a mere multi-millionaire. I can remember days when the maid and butler went without food."

Bill Wirtz loves to entertain friends and co-conspirators on his 124-foot yacht, the Blackhawk IV — named after the team's customary spot in the standings. The lavish vessel was custom built in the Netherlands, is docked off the coast of Florida, and features a hot tub, a formal dining room for eight, and a walk-in freezer that fits up to six Sutter brothers. Wirtz's yachtmates here include Bob Pulford (smiling) and Alan Eagleson (scheming). Tragically, the three have found themselves hopelessly lost at sea after mistakenly using Wirtz's moral compass.

*A picture, as they say, is worth a thousand lies,
especially when it's photo manipulated.

In January 1998, the reclusive Wirtz made his last public appearance at a Blackhawks event (the sold-out "Bob Probert Specimen Jar Giveaway Nite"). While there, Wirtz triumphantly flashed the number of Stanley Cups the Hawks have won since he took control of the team in 1967.

On May 3, 1972 Mayor Richard J. Daley, "America's Last Boss," and Arthur Wirtz, "The Baron of The Bottom Line" embraced one another after Wirtz endorsed Mayor Daley as "a friend of unprincipled, lawless monopolists everywhere." History records that the two men had a unique relationship: In exchange for large campaign contributions to Daley, Arthur got to feed the toes of his enemies to the seals in Lincoln Park Zoo.

In June 1976, Bill Wirtz signed Bobby Orr to a six-year, $3 million contract. "This is the big one we've been waiting for," Wirtz announced. "It's only a matter of time before Bobby Orr brings the Blackhawks a Stanley Cup. This day will be remembered as one of the proudest in Blackhawks history." It wasn't to be. Over the course of the next three seasons, Orr played a total of 26 games for the Blackhawks before retiring from the game permanently in 1978 due to knee injuries. Then Orr was forced to sue Wirtz for the guaranteed portion of his contract. In a revised statement, Wirtz announced: "Bobby Orr is a piece of shit."

In December 1995, Wirtz took a solemn oath promising to make Jeremy Roenick "a Blackhawk for life." (not pictured — crossed fingers.) *Editors' note*: This photo has become a collector's item in the market for one-of-a-kind sports memorabilia items, as it is a rare photo of Wirtz's hand that is usually only found in fans' pockets.

Bill Wirtz has long been a believer in the virtues of physical fitness. Here, Wirtz is seen training for his favorite road race, the Annual 5K Run For Tax Shelter Research. Other forms of exercise Bill enjoys include price-hiking, 12" political hardball and wrestling with his conscience.

In what was arguably the worst personnel decision in the history of professional sports, in 1972 Wirtz and his father Arthur allowed Bobby Hull to leave the Blackhawks for the WHA, claiming they did not want to upset the Blackhawks' salary structure. Bill Wirtz later admitted that letting Hull go was the "biggest mistake" he ever made. Here, in an effort at reconciliation, before a packed house at Chicago Stadium, Wirtz congratulates Hull on the retirement of his jersey and hairpiece.

Bill Wirtz is seen here reading his favorite self-help book. Whenever making difficult decisions, Wirtz routinely asks himself, "What Would Machiavelli Do?" Favorite passages from *The Prince* include: "Either be really nice to people or kill 'em'," "A gun is man's best friend," and "Morons televise their home games." Other favorites from the Wirtz library include *Tuesdays With Morrie The Accountant* and *The Collected Sales Receipts of Fandemonium, 1995-99.*

Desperately seeking aid for India's hungry and forgotten souls, Mother Theresa visited Bill Wirtz in Chicago on January 5, 1989. Deeply moved by Mother Theresa's appeals, Wirtz ordered an immediate air lift of three small Connie's Pizza to Calcutta (drinks sold separately).

Though often criticized for his lack of charitableness, Bill Wirtz was honored in 1997 by *Scotch Afficionado* magazine as their Humanitarian-of-the-Year for instituting the first Scotch-On-Wheels program for homebound alcoholics. Congratulations, Bill!

After years of trial and error, Bob Pulford demonstrates the best way to watch a Blackhawks hockey game.

Bill Wirtz and Bob Pulford meet on their favorite "horsey" to plot new ways of taking Hawks' fans for a ride. Wirtz seems to enjoy the ride as saddle-mate Pulford shows him exactly how it feels to be a Blackhawks' season-ticket holder.

In 1986, marketing geniuses Bill Wirtz and then NHL President John Ziegler receive a standing ovation at Chicago Stadium for making hockey the number 12 team sport in the United States, just behind pro beach volleyball.

Who needs a Stanley Cup parade? Bob Pulford supplies the human shield as Bill Wirtz waves to a cheering crowd of Wall Street bankers after winning the "Forbes Cup," given annually to the hockey franchise that loses the most games while generating the most revenue. (Photo courtesy Abraham Zapruder.)

Bill Wirtz amuses dinner companions with spot-on impersonation of an unscrupulous drunken bastard. Later, Wirtz displays his competitive side during drinking game called, "Pass Out and Vomit."

When asked after a recent NHL Board of Governors' meeting (September 2000) why a billionaire in the twilight of his years who has never won a Stanley Cup would still pinch pennies and bottom-line people to death, the Ka-ching of Hockey angrily replied: "Despite all the harsh public denunciations you people direct at me, I'll have you know that I am *not* engaged in the never-ending accumulation of massive wealth for my own selfish benefit. I'm engaged in the never-ending accumulation of massive wealth to benefit vitally important charities — my horse farm, my hedgefund, and my offshore bank!"

"It's unethical! It's despicable! It's vulgar!
Do I hear any objections?"

CHAPTER 5

Robbing the Public Purse

*"Some of the worst crimes people
commit are perfectly legal."*

— *Mark Weinberg*

On May 21, 1999, Illinois Governor George Ryan signed into law the Illinois Wine and Spirits Industry Fair Dealing Act of 1999. The law, better known as the "Wirtz Law" in recognition of Bill Wirtz's leading role in lobbying for its passage, was special interest legislation at its absolute worst. It was a classic example of how the powerful can use their money and legislative connections to enrich themselves at the public's expense. The law gave wholesale liquor distributor Judge & Dolph, Ltd., a wholly owned subsidiary of Wirtz Corp., a virtual monopoly on liquor distribution in Illinois. The foul-smelling details of the legislation and its passage are a lesson in honest graft — actions technically legal but nonetheless unseemly. The story is a familiar one: A politically-connected insider guarantees his corporation hundreds of millions of dollars in increased profits; a few politicians get big campaign contributions; and the rest of us get screwed.

DEAR ROCKY

The liquor industry is divided into three distinct segments — manufacturers (a.k.a. suppliers), distributors, and retailers. Most states strictly prohibit crossover between the three segments: a supplier cannot distribute its own liquor and a distributor cannot be involved in the retail trade. Judge &

Dolph, Ltd. is the largest liquor distributor in Illinois.[1] Purchased in 1947 by Arthur Wirtz, the company peddles the two best-selling liquors in Illinois, J & B scotch and Smirnoff vodka, as well as other popular brands such as Stolichnaya vodka (Zhamnov's favorite), Jose Cuervo tequila, and Bailey's Irish Cream. The Wirtz Corp., through its holdings of various liquor distributors in six states, is one of the leading liquor distributors in the entire country. Its Nevada operations sell 50 percent of the liquor and 30 percent of the wine consumed in Nevada. According to court records, it is estimated that for the year ended June 30, 1999, Wirtz's liquor distributorships earned revenues totaling some $750 million. And according to a deposition by Rocky Wirtz, Bill Wirtz's son and Judge & Dolph's president, roughly 45 percent of that income — $340 million — came from Judge & Dolph.[2]

But over the years, Wirtz's liquor distributorships have been hampered by threats of defection and accusations of poor service. For example, in 1985, after nearly 40 years together, one the the world's largest manufacturers of liquor, Seagram, fired DeLuca Liquor and Wine Ltd., a Wirtz-owned liquor distributor in Las Vegas. To replace Seagram, Wirtz's Las Vegas distributor signed another supplier of liquor, but a few months later was fired again by this new supplier for poor service. Similarly, in Illinois, various suppliers have been increasingly dissatisfied with the performance of Judge & Dolph's services. For example, Kendall-Jackson Wineries, one of the last family-owned wineries in the country, which makes some of the country's most popular wine, grew increasingly disappointed with Judge and Dolph's performance soon after it became their Illinois distributor in 1995. According to an internal Kendall-Jackson memorandum, Judge & Dolph was "laced with the 'good ol' boy' mentality" and its management exhibited a "reluctance to change."[3] (Sound familiar Hawks' fans?) To support these charges, Kendall-Jackson's Senior Vice-President Michael Haarstad stated under oath that Kendall-Jackson had attempted to work with Judge & Dolph "to improve

---

[1]According to *Crain's Chicago Business*, Judge & Dolph, Ltd. distributes 54% of the liquor and wine sold in Illinois. See Jeff Bordon, "Banks, Booze, Buildings, Blackhawks Too: Inside The World of Bill Wirtz," *Crain's Chicago Business*, April 14, 1997, p.1. But *Crain's* estimate might actually be on the high side. Estimates made in 1999 have Judge & Dolph distributing roughly 30% of the liquor and wine sold in Illinois. No one disputes, however, that Judge & Dolph is the largest liquor distributor in the state. There are three other big Illinois distributors: Romano Brothers Beverage Co., Union Beverage, and Hamburg Distributing. Together, these companies supply nearly all of the liquor sold statewide.

[2]Joseph T. Hallihan and Douglas Holt, "How The Wirtzes Sold Liquor Law," *Chicago Tribune*, Nov. 12, 1999, p. 1N. I am indebted to the work by Hallihan and Holt. Much of their work is incorporated here.

[3]*Id.*

Judge & Dolph's sales and distribution performance. Despite Kendall-Jackson's efforts, however, Judge & Dolph has failed to meet its sales volumes and distribution goals and has otherwise failed to perform to the satisfaction of Kendall-Jackson."[4] The owner of Kendall-Jackson, Jess Jackson, testified under oath that Rocky Wirtz was fully aware of Kendall-Jackson's disappointment. Jess Jackson testified that Rocky told him, "If we don't [improve distribution], you can have the brand back."[5] Taking Rocky at his word, on April 22, 1999, officials from Kendall-Jackson sent Rocky a "Dear Rocky" letter, in which they fired Judge & Dolph as their Illinois distributor. According to court filings, Kendall-Jackson accounted for three percent of Judge & Dolph's Illinois sales.[6]

Fearing the loss of any additional business, the Wirtzes put their clout and money behind an effort to pass a law that would prevent liquormakers from taking their business away from Judge & Dolph. The result was the Illinois Wine and Spirits Industry Fair Dealing Act of 1999. The law's declared purpose was "to promote the public's interest in fair, efficient, and competitive distribution of wine and liquor products."[7] But what the law actually did was lock in business for distributors such as Judge & Dolph by making it nearly impossible for liquormakers to break contracts and switch from one distributor to another. Passage of the law meant that suppliers could no longer play one distributor against another — the sort of honest competition every supplier or broker or middleman everywhere is subject to.

THE 'FRANCHISE FOREVER' LAW

What did the law say? How did it lock in business for Judge and Dolph? Why was the law called the "Franchise Forever" law? To begin with, the law was written in almost total secrecy, and it's no wonder: its provisions gave liquor distributors extraordinary and virtually unheard of powers.

First, the law forbade a liquormaker from canceling or not renewing a contract with its distributor, except for "good cause."[8] A seemingly benign phrase, "good cause" essentially meant a liquormaker could only change a distributor due to misconduct or non-performance. The decision to cancel or not renew could not be based on the legitimate business reasons of the liquor-

---

[4] Kendall-Jackson's Verified Amended Complaint; case No. 99-C-3813; filed June 21, 1999, paragraph 11.

[5] *Kendall-Jackson Winery, Ltd. v. Leonard L. Branson*, 2000 U.S. Dist Lexis 47 (January 3, 2000).

[6] *Id.*

[7] Illinois Wine and Spirits Industry Fair Dealing Act of 1999, §10.

[8] Illinois Wine and Spirits Industry Fair Dealing Act of 1999, §15.

maker itself, meaning a distributor like Judge & Dolph couldn't be fired for doing what the liquormaker considered to be a bad job, e.g., providing poor customer service or failing to promote efficient operations. The Chicago Office of the Federal Trade Commission argued that this "good faith" standard made it "virtually impossible" for a distributor to be fired.[9] Michael Binstein, chief executive officer of Binny's Beverage Depot, a 16-store Chicago-area retailer said, "It would take the equivalent of a Vatican annulment for a supplier to leave a wholesaler. They're married for life."[10]

Second, the law said that even if a distributor engaged in misconduct or failed to perform its duties, the distributor was granted 60 days to correct the deficiency. The law required a supplier to provide written notice of the supplier's intent to cancel or not renew a distribution agreement, and the notice must be sent 90 days before the supplier cancels or fails to renew. The notice must include a statement of reasons (including all necessary documentation) for the dismissal and must give the distributor 60 days to correct any claimed deficiency. If the deficiency is rectified within 60 days, the notice is void.[11]

Third, the law applied retroactively to contracts signed *before* the law was even passed! This betrayed the true purpose of the law, which was actually to protect the business interests of existing distributors rather than to promote the well-being of the liquor distribution industry in Illinois in general. Currently under Illinois law, a supplier is required to have an Illinois liquor distributor distribute its liquor. Any supplier who terminates a distribution contract is required to find another Illinois distributor, which means that Illinois jobs are not the issue here, only *particular* jobs for *particular* companies. In essence, what this law did was impose a freeze on existing relations. Incredibly, the retroactive portion of the law meant that a liquor supplier could not even take bids from various distributors before becoming locked in to that distributor's services.[12]

Fourth and finally, under the Wirtz Law, the legal process by which a supplier could actually remove a distributor for "good cause" was made ridiculously burdensome. The Illinois Liquor Control Commission (ILCC), the administrative body overseeing the sale of liquor in Illinois, was given the authority to order a dissatisfied liquor supplier to continue providing liquor to a distributor who failed to perform its services. If a liquor supplier challenged the ILCC's order by appealing to a federal or state court, the ILCC's

---

[9]Douglas Holt, "Liquor Barons Tack On Price Hike," *Chicago Tribune*, June 25, 1999, p. 1N.
[10]*Id.*
[11]See Illinois Wine and Spirits Industry Fair Dealing Act of 1999, § 20.
[12]*Id* at §10(d).

order remained in effect until the matter was determined by a court order that was "final and non-reviewable."[13] This "final and non-reviewable" provision meant that the ILCC's order remained binding until all appeals were exhausted, even if a federal or state court reversed the ILCC's order. Thus, the ILCC's order continued in effect until the case had been heard in every possible higher court, a process that would likely take years to complete.

In response to the passage of the Wirtz Law, angry editorials appeared in every major Chicago paper. The *Chicago Tribune* called the law "anti-consumer," "special-interest, monopoly-building legislation" that "plays favorites among business interests" and allows liquor distributors to engage in "price-gouging."[14] The *Sun-Times* condemned the law as "anathema to a free-market," noting the law guarantees that "Wirtz and his family" will "remain" "the state's largest liquor distributorship."[15] And the *Chicago Daily Herald* called the law "unconscionable," "a bad law that protects one business at the expense of competitors and consumers alike," "creat[ing] an unfair monopoly" and "prohibit[ing] wine and liquor makers from firing their distributors."[16]

ROCKY AND HOODWINKLE

In defense of the law, Rocky Wirtz stated that it was needed to "protect Illinois jobs."[17] Bill Wirtz's spokesman, Guy Chipparoni, accused the liquor-makers of trying to "completely control a local market at the expense of jobs."[18] A massive public relations campaign was organized to present this special-interest legislation as a jobs protection program, including having Judge & Dolph employees meet Illinois lawmakers in the halls of their Capitol offices bearing a special gift: a box of Frango mints. The candies, which had been made in the kitchen of the Marshall Field's store in down-

---

[13]*Id.* at §35(c)(2).

[14]Editorial, "Repeal The Liquor Monopoly," *Chicago Tribune*, July 18, 1999, p. 16c.

[15]Editorial, "Law Without Merit," *Chicago Sun-Times*, Jan. 11, 2000, p. 21.

[16]Editorial, "Flawed Liquor Law Finally On The Rocks" *Chicago Daily Herald*, January 27, 2000, p.14N.

[17]Douglas Holt, "If Wirtz Law Falls, Liquor Price May Not," *Chicago Tribune*, January 5, 2000, p. 1N.

[18]Douglas Holt, *Chicago Tribune*, June 25, 1999, p. 1N. It is interesting to note that throughout the whole lobbying effort to pass this legislation, Bill Wirtz himself was completely silent. Wirtz never once uttered a public word about the bill, employing spokesmen and lobbyists and middlemen: "He shows them the goal, provides the money, insists on results, but vehemently declines to know the foul methods by which alone his understappers get...'results.' Not to bribe, but to employ and finance the briber; not to lie but to reward the liar; not to commit perjury but to hire men to protect him from the reaches of the law." E.A. Ross, *Sin and Society,* New York, Haughton Mifflin (1907) p. 52.

town Chicago since 1929, were a potent political symbol. In the spring of 1999, Marshall Field's owner, Minneapolis-based Dayton Hudson Corp., closed the Marshall Field's kitchen, sending the work out of state, which cost Illinois 157 jobs. The decision caused an uproar, and Dayton Hudson was vilified as an uncaring, out-of-state conglomerate. And just in case the lawmakers missed the symbolism of the mints, they were accompanied with a note asking for a favorable vote on the Fair Dealing Act, "to ensure that my job doesn't end like the hard working Frango mint workers."[19]

But the jobs argument was public relations hokum. The Fair Dealing Act did nothing to protect Illinois jobs. Under pre-existing Illinois law, the liquor-makers were required to employ an Illinois distributor to distribute their liquor. As a vestige of post-Prohibition days, Illinois had adopted the three-tier system of liquor distribution, in which there exists liquor suppliers, wholesale distributors and liquor retailers. Fearing that producers would monopolize markets, lawmakers had set up strict divisions among these groups. Thus, a supplier cannot legally operate in Illinois without an *independent* Illinois distributor. A supplier's termination of one distributor means it *must* hire another. So in reality the Wirtz Law did nothing to create or protect jobs; it simply froze existing relationships, thus aiding specific distributors.

THE LAW'S EFFECT? HIGHER PRICES...DUH

The immediate effect of the Wirtz Law was increased prices for consumers. Only days after the law took effect, Judge & Dolph provoked outrage when it raised prices to retailers three percent to six percent — an increase that was settled on after the threat of far bigger increases elicited a public scolding from Governor George Ryan.[20] To justify the price increases, Judge and Dolph stated that it needed to raise prices to counter the increase in the State liquor tax effective July 1, 1999. In separate legislation, lawmakers had approved a liquor tax hike that increased the tax rate for beer six cents a six-pack, a dime to an average bottle of wine and about 50 cents to a fifth of hard liquor.[21] But a *Chicago Tribune* investigation revealed that Judge & Dolph actually raised prices 2 1/2 times the increase in the new liquor tax. A spot check of grocery stores showed that a fifth of Jack Daniel's had jumped $2.00 to $15.99 and a bottle of Kendell-Jackson chardonnay had zoomed $2.00 to $13.99.[22] Wirtz was using the liquor tax as a cover to impose his own price

[19]Joseph T. Hallihan and Douglas Holt, *Chicago Tribune*, Nov. 12, 1999, p. 1N.

[20]See Douglas Holt, *Chicago Tribune*, September 25, 1999, p. 1N.

[21]The tax increase was passed as part of Governor George Ryan's $12 billion so-called Illinois FIRST program to renovate the state's infrastructure.

[22]See Douglas Holt, *Chicago Tribune*, September 25, 1999, p. 1N.

increases. The hope was that consumers would believe the increase was due to the tax hike and that the money would be going for schools and roads rather than in the pockets of the distributors themselves. According to Steve Reidl, executive director of the Illinois Licensed Beverage Association, which represents liquor retailers, the price increase implemented by the Wirtzes produced an additional $30 million in revenue for Wirtz and his fellow liquor distributors.[23]

Everyone knew this law would be bad for consumers. Higher prices was the only logical outcome. In March 1999, while the legislature was "debating" the Wirtz bill, C. Steven Baker, director of the Chicago office of the Federal Trade Commission, warned lawmakers that the measure would "shield the business of liquor distribution from market forces" and would have the likely result of "increased consumer prices."[24] Even an unpublished confidential House Republican memorandum written before the law was passed concluded that the Wirtz bill would likely increase prices for consumers.[25] The law removed any restraint on distributors from raising their prices, since they could no longer be fired for raising them or for not meeting their sales targets. As the *Chicago Daily Herald* explained, "Normally, of course, a producer would seek out the distributor that could do the best job at the lowest cost. But because the law guaranteed it clients and protected it from competitive pressures, Judge & Dolph was free to raise prices."[26]

VOTE BUYING 101

So how did Wirtz do it? How did he go about purchasing self-aggrandizing, special-interest, monopoly-building legislation that guaranteed his family millions of dollars in additional profits at the expense of consumer interests? No need to phone a friend here — the answer is easy: with lots of money and lots of lobbyists. According to the *Chicago Daily Herald*, the bill was the result of one of Illinois' most "well-financed and successful lobbying blitzes" in history.[27] The *Chicago Tribune* described it as the result of "persistent and extraordinary intense lobbying orchestrated by Chicago Blackhawks' owner Bill Wirtz."[28]

[23]Douglas Holt, "Judge Puts Wirtz Liquor Law On Hold," *Chicago Tribune*, Jan. 4, 2000, p. 1N.

[24]Ray Long and Douglas Holt, "2nd Leapfrog Liquor Hike Possible," *Chicago Tribune*, Nov. 25, 1999, p. 1N.

[25]Rich Miller, "The Money Grab," *The Capitol Fax*, Dec. 3, 1998, p. 1.

[26]Editorial, *Chicago Daily Herald*, January 27, 2000, p. 14N.

[27]Don Thompson, "Money Flowed With Liquor Bill Blackhawks Owner," *Chicago Daily Herald*, November 5, 1999, p. 11N.

[28]Editorial, "Repeal The Liquor Monopoly," *Chicago Tribune*, July 18, 1999, p. 16c.

The Fair Dealing Act made its debut in the state legislature in December 1998, accompanied by some of the most powerful men in Springfield. According to state records, Wirtz Corp. hired 28 lobbyists, including former Governor "Big" Jim Thompson and former Senate President Phil "Pet" Rock. At the same time, Wirtz started making large contributions to those politicians best positioned to help get the law enacted — namely, the top leaders in the Illinois House and Senate, as well as George Ryan, then the Republican nominee for governor. Public records reveal that Wirtz poured more than $300,000 into the coffers of various lawmakers in the months before they considered the Fair Dealing Act, including money funneled through the family's out-of-state businesses.[29]

Specifically, on Monday, May 11, 1998, five out-of-state liquor distributors owned by Bill Wirtz all made identical $10,000 contributions to the gubernatorial campaign of George Ryan, who was then secretary of state.[30] Rocky Wirtz added $1,000 of his own money; Bill Wirtz added $1,000 of his own money; and Judge & Dolph threw in an additional $250. In all, Ryan received $52,250 in a matter of a few days from the Wirtzes.

[29]To understand the ins-and-outs of vote-buying in Illinois, it is necessary to explain how power is distributed in the Illinois legislature. In Illinois, power is concentrated at the top — the two party leaders in the Senate and the two party leaders in the House control almost all the money raised and they then funnel it towards the candidates of their choice. Thus, the trick to buying legislation is to buy off the big guys, since they are the ones who control the legislative agenda. The four big shots, often referred to as the "four tops," are the majority leader of the House, House Speaker Michael Madigan; the minority leader of the House, Rep. Lee Daniels; the majority leader of the Senate, Senate President James "Pate" Philip; and the minority leader of the Senate, Sen. Emil Jones, Jr. In 1998, a typical year, records show that Speaker Madigan raised $4.1 million; Minority Leader Daniels $7.5 million; Senate President Philip $4.8 million; and Minority Leader Jones $2.2 million. The four legislative leaders then dole out their war chests to candidates of their choice. They alone determine which races will be battlegrounds during the campaigns. In 1998, in all House races for the Illinois legislature, the average Republican spent $319,000, and 67 percent of that, or $215,000, was given to the House candidate by the Republican legislative leaders. Likewise, the average Democrat running for the House in 1998 spent $253,000, and 68 percent of that, or $171,000, was provided by the funds from the two Democratic legislative leaders. Based on these realities, it is unsurprising that the vast majority of money given by Wirtz to pass this law was given to these four legislative leaders, as well as to then gubernatorial candidate George Ryan. (Records made available to the author by The Sunshine Project, a non-profit research institute based in Springfield, Illinois, whose objective is increasing public awareness of the role of money in Illinois politics.)

[30]The five out-of-state liquor distributors that contributed are: Griggs and Cooper, a Wirtz-owned liquor distributor in Minnesota; Edison Liquor Corp., a Wirtz-owned liquor distributor in Wisconsin; DeLuca Liquor and Wine Ltd., a Wirtz-owned liquor distributor in Las Vegas; Longhorn Liquors Ltd., a Wirtz-owned liquor distributor in Texas; and Silver State Liquor & Wine, Inc., a second Wirtz-owned liquor distributor in Nevada.

These contributions were soon followed by donations to key legislators: On Sept. 15, 1998, Judge & Dolph gave $10,000 to the campaign of Senate Minority Leader Emil Jones, Jr. On Oct. 2, DeLuca Liquor & Wine gave $15,000 to House Republican Leader Lee Daniels, and that same day Edison Liquor Corp. gave Daniels an additional $10,000. On Oct. 4, House Speaker Michael Madigan received $10,000 from Longhorn Liquors, plus $15,000 from Silver State Liquor & Wine, Inc. Finally, on Oct. 13, Griggs, Cooper & Co. gave $10,000 to Senate President James "Pate" Philip.

In total, the Wirtzes and their corporate entities contributed $122,250 in the months before the Fair Dealing Act was introduced. According to State Board of Elections records, that is nearly double the amount they had contributed to the state's politicians in the previous four years combined.[31]

But these numbers aren't an accurate indication of the actual amount of money Wirtz was passing around. Those numbers simply reflect the money that can be tracked to Wirtz-owned companies. It ignores the money given by Wirtz-controlled political action committees (PACs).

Public records reveal that the Wirtz-controlled IWAPAC gave $233,432 in 1997 and 1998 in contributions to Illinois politicians. IWA stands for the Illinois Wholesale (liquor) Association PAC. IWAPAC is the PAC of the Wine and Spirits Distributors of Illinois, a 27-member trade group for distributors, which Wirtz controls.[32] The IWA did not exist prior to December 1997 and there was very little money given to Illinois politicians before 1998 by the Wine and Spirits Distributors of Illinois. One can only conclude that its creation was tied directly to the Wirtz Bill.

In 1997 and 1998, IWAPAC gave $10,000 to House Republican Leader Lee Daniels; $6,500 to Emil Jones; $4,300 to George Ryan; $6,000 to James "Pate" Philips; $15,000 to House Speaker Michael Madigan. Then in 1999, the IWAPAC gave another $10,000 to Governor Ryan; another $10,000 to Emil Jones; another $5,000 to Lee Daniels; another $10,500 to Mike Madigan. The IWA also spread around an additional $67,897 to other, less influential politicians in 1998.

[31]See Joseph T. Hallihan and Douglas Holt, *Chicago Tribune*, Nov. 12, 1999, p. 1N.

[32]It is impossible to know precisely how much either Wirtz individually or Judge & Dolph as an entity contributed to the IWAPAC in comparison to contributions from other IWAPAC members. In its report for the second half of 1998, the IWAPAC campaign contributions reports changed from listing contributions from individual distributors to listing lump sum transfers from the Wine and Spirits Distributors of Illinois to the IWAPAC. According to University of Illinois at Springfield Professor Kent Redfield, who heads The Sunshine Project, a research group that monitors Illinois campaign contributions, this practice is "a violation of the spirit, if not the letter, of Illinois' campaign disclosure laws." Mr. Redfield has raised the issue with the State Board of Elections, but nothing has happened yet. Personal conversation between the author and Kent Redfield on July 29, 2000.

But even this doesn't reveal the true extent of Wirtz's spending spree. The contributions mentioned so far only concern money given to individual legislators and ignores contributions given to the general funds controlled by the Democratic and Republican leaders in both the House and Senate, as well as contributions made to the Illinois Democratic and Republican parties. When looking at how much a leader got or how much money he controls, one has to consider both the leader's personal committee and their parties' committees. Public records reveal that in late 1997 and 1998, Wirtz-controlled entities gave $13,700 to the Senate Republicans, $3,500 to Senate Democrats, $26,650 to House Republicans, $22,800 to House Democrats, and $6,000 to the Illinois State Democratic Party, for a total of another $72,650.

When you add it all up, Wirtz's total contributions from 1997 to mid-1999 were $309,650. Not a bad investment when you consider, as the *Chicago Tribune* did, that as a result of the Wirtz Law, "The Wirtz family stands to make millions of dollars in Illinois while facing almost no competition."[33] Even this hefty sum, however, almost surely underreports Wirtz's total contributions. The reason is that certain modes of making political contributions make it virtually impossible to trace the money. For example, political donations are often made through hired lobbyists on their client's behalf. The contributions are given in the lobbyist's own name, and the client is then billed for them as part of the overall cost of the lobbying effort. The politicians know the money's true source, but the public record is obscured.[34]

DENYING THE OBVIOUS

American politicians and their patrons know what to do in the face of legislative vote buying: deny it! And that's exactly what they did here. Asked whether the contributions were related to the Fair Dealing Act, Rocky Wirtz said, "No. Absolutely not. All we wanted to do was put some sanity back in Illinois."[35] Asked if the Wirtz money had any influence on him, George Ryan

---

[33]Joseph T. Hallihan and Douglas Holt, *Chicago Tribune*, Nov. 12, 1999, p. 1N.

[34]Still another effective but rather mundane way to influence legislators is by wining and dining them. One evening in early 1999 Wirtz and his lobbyists entertained a group of 45 lawmakers with dinner and cocktails. The tab for the night came to $2,666.00. Similarly, in 1999, public records reveal that Wirtz lobbyist W. Michael McCreery gave Republican leaders Lee Daniels and James Philips gifts of Huntingware outdoor garments. See Christi Parsons, "Wirtz's Team Effort Listed Among Lobbyist Records," *Chicago Tribune*, February 2, 1999, p. 1N. And in Springfield, Wirtz is well known and much loved for his generosity regarding free Blackhawks tickets. One public official told *Chicago Magazine*, "Legislatures were always saying that when they needed Hawks tickets, they'd phone the CEO [Wirtz]." Lisa Twyman Bessone, "Power Play," *Chicago Magazine*, January, 1992, p. 89.

[35]Joseph T. Hallihan and Douglas Holt, *Chicago Tribune*, Nov. 12, 1999, p. 1N.

said: "[The Wirtz contributions] didn't have any influence on me."[36] Senate Republican Spokeswoman Patty Schuh told the *Chicago Daily Herald*, "[The Wirtz] campaign contributions do not influence members of this body." Ms. Schuh insisted that contributors give to lawmakers who reflect their overall views and philosophy, not to influence a vote on any particular piece of legislation.[37] In fact, however, there was no ideological design to the money given by Wirtz. The two parties more or less split the loot, with both right-wing and left-wing members in each party getting their fair share.

And if the passage of the law was truly on the up-and-up and in the public interest, why all the secretiveness about it? One of the many suspicious aspects here is Wirtz's out-of-state campaign contributions from his distributorships in Minnesota, Nevada, Texas, and Wisconsin. Unlike under federal law, in Illinois there are no limits to campaign contributions. Anyone — a person, a corporation, a PAC, even a Blackhawks' fan — can give money in Illinois, and they can give as much as they want. Illinois is one of only two states in the nation with no limits on campaign contributions. (The other is Texas.) Since the Wirtzes could easily have given the money from their own pocketbook or from their in-state distributorship, the question is, why did they orchestrate an effort to funnel hundreds of thousands of dollars through their out-of-state corporations?

The answer is obvious. Giving the money from out-of-state corporations provided a better way to hide the extent of their contributions. It was a way to avoid raising eyebrows. As University of Illinois Professor Kent Redfield, who heads the Sunshine Project, a research institute in Springfield, Illinois that monitors the role of money in Illinois politics, explained: "Because there is no prohibition on direct corporate giving and no limit on how much any individual, group, or entity can give in Illinois, the only reason I can think of to give through the out-of-state companies is to hide or obscure the true source of the contributions. By using hidden contributions, special interests like Wirtz are able to fly below the radar screen of public disclosure laws."[38] The stealth donations weren't the only indication the parties involved knew this legislation stunk to high heaven. The legislation itself was passed in a manner suggesting the same. The law was passed on the last

[36]Jon Kass, "Big-Game Hunter Seemingly Content With Tiny Takedowns," *Chicago Tribune*, November 15, 1999, p. 3N.

[37]Don Thompson, "Money Flowed With Liquor Bill Blackhawks Owner," *Chicago Daily Herald,* November 5, 1999, p. 11N. Frankly, instead of being so defensive about their support of the Wirtz Law, the Republicans may have been better off embracing the bill and coining a spankin' new campaign slogan — "A Thousand Pints of Lite!"

[38]Personal conversation between the author and Kent Redfield on July 29, 2000.

day of the legislative session on May 20, 1999, and as the *Chicago Tribune* observed, Governor Ryan waited only a day to sign it, "announcing the action at 4:30 p.m. on a Friday in an effort to avoid publicity."[39]

DEGRADATION OF THE
POLITICAL PROCESS, PART #4,975

The issues surrounding the passage of the Wirtz Law are of course bigger than Bill Wirtz himself. It's not exactly news that politicians have grown more and more dependent on "gifts" from wealthy individuals and corporate interests. Due to the huge sums of money necessary to run for office, our system bends over backward to indulge big donors and their special interests. But even recognizing such political realities, there is still a line separating unreasonable from reasonable uses of economic power and political clout. This line is sometimes hard to define, but the Wirtz Law crossed any reasonable boundary. The law did not serve the public interest in *any* fashion. The law eliminated competition in the liquor distribution business, locked in a monopoly for Wirtz's company, and freed Wirtz to raise prices with near impunity. You don't have to be a spit-foaming Bolshevik to wonder about a legislative process in which wealthy corporate interests can purchase this sort of self-aggrandizing legislation.

Moreover, the so-called legislative leaders responsible for pushing this law through the backdoor seem to have lost any sense of the proper line between a law fostering the general public interest and one fostering the narrow interests of those with money. House Speaker Michael Madigan justified the legislation by saying, "They're citizens of this state too."[40] Well, yes, Mr. Speaker, they certainly are, but your defense of the Wirtz Law justifies any and all special-interest legislation, no matter how self-serving and no matter how contrary to the public interest, for all special-interest legislation is done for the benefit of somebody's interest, presumably a citizen of the State. Madigan's defense also turns language on its head, for by presenting this law as a responsible act of public policy it turns the taking of a political bribe, here called a campaign contribution, into some kind of virtuous act of public service.

Meanwhile, Senate President James "Pate" Philips took a different tack to justify the law. He defended the Wirtz Law by misrepresenting it as nothing but an innocent and benign measure. Ignoring the true language and effects of the law, Philips disingenuously told the *Chicago Tribune*, "This

---

[39]Ray Long and Rick Pearson, "Springfield Success Stories That's Rich," *Chicago Tribune*, May 29, 1999, p. 1N.

[40]*Id.*

doesn't guarantee these guys [business] forever. That's a lot of baloney. All we said is, 'Before you take the franchise, you have to show cause.' What's wrong with that?"[41] But everyone knew this law locked in liquor manufacturers to their distributors. That was the law's very point. Philips' misrepresentation of the law's effect actually betrays the crime itself: You don't have to lie about a law you're proud of.

Finally, former Illinois Governor Jim Thompson, now a lobbyist for the law firm of Winston & Strawn, who was hired by Wirtz to insure passage of the law, also feebly defended it. Thompson didn't deny that the law was anything other than rank special-interest legislation; instead, he dismissed the whole issue of special-interest legislation as unimportant. "I know you guys love to obsess over the Wirtz bill and gambling and all that stuff. But to the average guy in the state of Illinois, it's meaningless,"[42] Thompson asserted. Meaningless? It's true there weren't protests in the streets over passage of the Wirtz Law, but the absence of public outrage doesn't mean the public wasn't disgusted by it. Jim Howard, executive director of Illinois Common Cause, put it this way: "Unfortunately, the vast majority of citizens have decided not to pay attention to government because they feel they can no longer affect public policy. The reason is that your average citizen all too often sees millionaires — or in this case billionaires — walking away with everything they want courtesy of our legislators."[43]

We live in an age of political passivity, even cynicism, but Jim Thompson's attitude is the height of that cynicism. One might expect a former governor to have a bit loftier notion of public service and the public good than what the public will tolerate without protest. A somnolent public is no reason to rip them off. Not only does Thompson refuse to acknowledge the dangers inherent in the *appearance* of influence peddling; he refuses to acknowledge the dangers in *actual* influence peddling. Needless to say, Thompson's efforts to pooh-pooh the significance of this legislation is highly self-serving. As an ex-government-official-turned-high-priced-lawyer-lobbyist, Thompson earns his living by helping pass this type of legislation. He thus has a vested interest in minimizing its ugliness. For as long as the public puts up with it, Thompson can ply his trade with impunity.

---

[41]Ray Long and Joseph T. Hallihan, "Philip Wants To Let Courts Sort Out Liquor Law," *Chicago Tribune*, Jan. 26, 2000, p. 1N.

[42]Ray Long and Rick Pearson, "Springfield Success Stories That's Rich," *Chicago Tribune*, May 29, 1999, p. 1N.

[43]Personal conversation between author and Jim Howard on October 11, 2000. In reference to the large sums of money Wirtz threw at various Illinois politicians to pass this law, Mr. Howard said, "Bill Wirtz looked like a man waving his wallet to a street walker."

TAKE IT TO THE JUDGE

On January 3, 2000, just six months after the Wirtz Law was passed, U.S. District Judge Joan B. Gottschall issued a preliminary injunction that blocked the state from enforcing the Wirtz Law after three large wineries challenged the law in court.[44] The judge ruled that the law violated the Commerce Clause and the Contracts Clause of the U.S. Constitution and was in direct conflict with established Illinois law. The judge's decision meant the Wirtz Law became effectively unenforceable. In response to the judge's harsh condemnation of the law, Governor Ryan announced that the state would not defend the law in the appellate courts, thus tacitly acknowledging the law's unconstitutionality and ending its life.[45]

In the end, Bill Wirtz didn't get his liquor monopoly, and he must now compete for business like all the rest of us. But don't cry for Bill. He was foiled here, but he'll be back. The Wirtz Law is just one of many examples of Wirtz's buying special-interest legislation over the years. "Like it or not," *Chicago Magazine* concluded a few years back, "Wirtz can pretty much do as he damn well pleases [in the legislature]."[46] Another instance of his influence peddling occurred in 1986, when Bismarck Food Services (now called Bismarck Enterprises), a Wirtz-family owned entity, was awarded the Chicago Park District's concession contract, a 10-year deal worth at least $58 million.[47] Similarly, in 1994, upon the opening of the renovated Navy Pier, Pier Management Services, an affiliate of Bismarck Enterprises, was awarded the exclusive contract to operate the food concessions business at the Pier.[48]

In addition, prior to the opening of the United Center in 1994, Wirtz and his partner Jerry Reinsdorf had arranged huge special tax breaks for the United Center thanks to a bill passed in the Illinois legislature. The tax breaks meant that the United Center would pay only a fraction of what other similar commercial properties pay, saving Wirtz and Reinsdorf tens of millions of dollars in real estate taxes over a period of 24 years.[49] What this all means, of course, is that Bill Wirtz can now deduct the cost of being chauffeured to

[44]*Kendall-Jackson Winery, Ltd., v. Leonard L. Branson*, 2000 U.S. Dist Lexis 47 (January 3, 2000).

[45] Douglas Holt, *Chicago Tribune*, June 25, 1999, p. 1N.

[46]Lisa Twyman Bessone, "Power Play," *Chicago Magazine*, January, 1992, p. 89.

[47]John McCarron, "A Park Plum For Wirtz-Run Firm," *Chicago Tribune*, April 22, 1986, p. 3C.

[48]Fran Spielman, "Council Moves to Get Pier Its Liquor Quicker," *Chicago Sun-Times*, June 10, 1995, p. 3.

[49]By way of comparison, the Presidential Towers, an apartment and commercial complex built in Chicago for approximately the same cost as the United Center ($180 million),

every Blackhawks game so he can sit in his tax-deductible skybox in the stadium on which he pays minimal property taxes, all the while wining and dining politicians for the purpose of receiving even more perks from the state in the future.

"Behind every great fortune is a crime," wrote Balzac. Had he been writing about Bill Wirtz, he might have said, behind every great fortune lies a sweet deal with spineless, money-hungry politicians. And don't think Bill Wirtz doesn't know it. It's been said that Bill Wirtz has gotten everything he's ever wanted from the Mayor Daley — well, strictly speaking, the conventional political wisdom has it that Bill Wirtz has never *not* gotten something that he's really wanted from Mayor Daley. In appreciation of this, Bill Wirtz in 1994 said that he would never do anything to affront Mayor Daley: "My father used to have an expression: 'Don't hit Santa Claus,' and he was right. The mayor's been wonderful to us."[50]

---

pays $5 million a year in taxes, whereas the United Center pays just $1 million. Instead of letting the Cook County assessor value the United Center as he does all other properties, the legislature tied the assessor's hands and took the highly unusual step of setting the taxes on the stadium for him. See Chuck Neubauer, "Stadium Snares Huge Tax Breaks Under State Law," *Chicago Sun-Times*, April 16, 1995, p. 16N (the article describes the rather complicated formula for figuring the United Center's annual taxes).

[50]Fran Spielman, "The Puck Stops Here; Bill Wirtz Gives Family New Legacy With Stadium," *Chicago Sun-Times*, August 28, 1994, p.1.

"No, no, Bill...Believe me, the pleasure was *all* mine."

CHAPTER 6

Cheating the NHL Players' Association

"I will live up to both responsibilities."

— *Jimmy Hoffa, when asked at Congressional Hearings if he realized what power he could wield as president of the Teamsters, for good or evil.*

Bill Wirtz served as the head of the NHL Board of Governors for 18 years from 1974 until 1992. During that time, he was the most powerful man in hockey — the Governors run the league, and Wirtz ran the Governors. For better or worse, Wirtz put his mark on every aspect of the NHL. As former NHL President John Ziegler declared, "No other NHL owner has been as significant in the development of this league as Bill Wirtz."[1] On the worse side, evidence suggests that during his tenure Wirtz conspired with convicted felon, Alan Eagleson, erstwhile head of the National Hockey League Players Association (NHLPA), to illegally enhance the owners' bargaining power against the players, including suppressing NHL player salaries and reducing players' pension benefits. There is currently a federal class-action lawsuit on the matter brought by several former NHL players.[2] The lawsuit alleges that, in exchange for illegal payments engineered by Wirtz, Eagleson agreed to sell-out the NHL players at the negotiating table.

---

[1]Herb Gould, "In a League By Himself," *Chicago Sun-Times*, February 5, 1992, p. 92.

[2]*Forbes et al v. Alan Eagleson et al*, Eastern District of Pennsylvania, No. 95-CV-7021. The five former NHL Players named as the plaintiffs in the suit are Dave Forbes formerly of the Boston Bruins, Brad Park formerly of the New York Rangers, Rick Middleton formerly of the Bruins, Ulf Nilsson formerly of the Rangers, and Doug Smail formerly of the Winnipeg Jets. The suit was brought as a class action on behalf of all players employed by NHL teams between 1975 and 1990.

The players are seeking hundreds of million in damages from the defendants. Wirtz may or may not be found guilty of the alleged crimes, but there is no question that this matter fits in with a *modus operandi* we have seen before — winning not through fair and honest means but with a sleeveful of aces.

THE EAGLE HAS LANDED...IN JAIL

Most hockey fans are familiar with Alan Eagleson. He ran the NHL players' union for 24 years from 1967 until 1991. Then after a four-year investigation by law-enforcement authorities in both the United States and Canada, Eagleson pled guilty on January 6, 1998 to three counts of mail fraud in a Boston courtroom and the next day to three additional counts of fraud in a Toronto courtroom.[3] For his crimes, Eagleson was fined $1 million (Cdn.) and sentenced to 18 months in prison. He was also drop-kicked out of the Hockey Hall-of-Fame, disbarred from practicing law in Canada and stripped of the prestigious Order of Canada.[4] The investigations revealed that Eagleson defrauded the players' pension fund, defrauded individual players, and made close to $3.5 million in illegal loans to family and friends from the players' own funds.

Eagleson was also shown to have illegally reaped enormous profits for himself by skimming money off the top and taking kickbacks in connection with various international hockey tournaments. As FBI agent Tom Daly, who lead the U.S. government's pursuit of Eagleson, put it, "If there was a way you could skim it, Alan found it."[5] The investigations also revealed evidence that Eagleson was in collusion with the NHL owners to sell-out NHL players at the bargaining table in exchange for control over international hockey. The details of Eagleson's crimes as head of the NHLPA have been fully documented by others.[6] But Bill Wirtz's roll in the commission of Eagleson's crimes has been less appreciated. The goal of this chapter is to show that Bill Wirtz worked hand-in-hand with Eagleson to screw the NHLPA.

---

[3]This was plea bargained down from the original 32-count indictment that included charges of racketeering, embezzlement, kickbacks, mail fraud, and obstruction of justice.

[4]A truly impressive hat trick! The Order of Canada is Canada's highest civilian honor. Since 1967, the Order of Canada has recognized people who have made a difference to the nation in various areas, including the arts, politics, sports, business, and social justice.

[5]John Anderson, "Thin Ice," *The American Lawyer*, June 1998, p. 57.

[6]For the blow-by-blow report of the crimes and corruption of Alan Eagleson as head of the NHLPA, see the indispensable work by Russ Conway, *Game Misconduct: Alan Eagleson and the Corruption of Hockey*, MacFarlane Walters & Ross, Toronto, 1995. Conway is the reporter responsible for first exposing Eagleson's wrongdoing. As a sup-

The fact is, none of Eagleson's crimes related to his control of international hockey could have occurred without the tacit consent of Bill Wirtz. As chairman of the NHL Board of governors for eighteen years, Wirtz acted as the chief negotiator for the NHL opposite of Eagleson in all negotiations between the league and its players, and in that capacity, Wirtz colluded *with* Eagleson against the players. Indeed, as the players' lawsuit makes clear, it was only through the good graces of Wirtz that Eagleson gained control of international hockey and its tournament proceeds. And while it's true that there exists no "smoking gun," that is, any written documentation, that proves Wirtz handed Eagleson international hockey on a silver platter in exchange for selling out the players, the *quid pro quo* is there for all to see in the way Eagleson served the interests of the NHL owners during his tenure as head of the NHLPA and in the extraordinary efforts the NHL took to keep Eagleson in power and stonewall efforts to discover and expose Eagleson's corrupt activities.

At the outset, it should be made clear that Wirtz and Eagleson were and are close friends. Both had vacation homes near each other in Florida (until, that is, the U.S. Justice Department appropriated Eagleson's U.S. home as part of his plea bargain with the government.) According to Gil Stein, former general counsel to the NHL and former interim president of the NHL, Eagleson and Wirtz "partied before and after collective bargaining sessions."[7] Even today, after Eagleson pleaded guilty to his various crimes, Wirtz dismisses the charges, saying, "Don't believe anything you hear and read about Alan. He'll be out of jail in fairly short order and more of the real truth will come out. I have no hesitation standing by his side."[8] In defense of Eagleson, Wirtz even permitted Hawks' GM Bob Pulford, also an old crony of Eaglesons, to submit a letter on Blackhawks' stationary on behalf of Eagleson to the judge at Eagleson's sentencing hearing in an effort to lighten his jail sentence. In the letter, Pulford recounts his own dealings with Eagleson and calls Eagleson's integrity "unquestionable." (A copy of this letter is provided in the Appendix.)

EAGLESON + WIRTZ = VILE CORRUPTION

During his reign as executive director of the NHLPA, Eagleson virtually single-handedly operated the union's daily affairs, conducting all the players' collective bargaining negotiations with the NHL. He also engaged in busi-

---

plement to Conway's work, see William Houston and David Shoalts, *Greed and Glory: The Fall of Hockey Czar Alan Eagleson*, Warwick Publishing, Inc., Toronto, 1993.

[7]John Anderson, *The American Lawyer* at 65.

[8]Howard Berger, "Wirtz Assails Canadians for Abandoning Eagleson." *The Toronto Globe and Mail*, January 23, 1998, Sports, p. 2.

ness activities for himself, working as a player agent and lawyer representing players and management personnel in their individual contract negotiations with club owners. And then, beginning in the mid-1970s and continuing through 1991, Eagleson was also responsible for organizing a number of international hockey tournaments, including the famed Canada Cup. Ostensibly, these tournaments were conducted under the auspices of a not-for-profit corporation called Hockey Canada, a quasi-governmental body. Hockey Canada had been formed in the 1960s to oversee and promote amateur hockey in Canada and over the years received millions of dollars in appropriations from the Canadian parliament for its operations.

Teams from European countries, Canada and the United States played in these international tournaments. The Canadian and U.S. teams consisted primarily of the NHL's best players. Without these stars, the tournaments could not have been financially successful because they would not have drawn a large enough audience. But because NHL players were prohibited by their contracts from playing on teams other than those of their employers, Eagleson needed the NHL owners' permission to obtain the players' services.

According to Eagleson's own 1991 autobiography, *Power Play*, it was Bill Wirtz himself who handed the control of international hockey to Eagleson. In 1976, there was much dispute among NHL owners about loaning NHL players to the 1976 Canada Cup. Gil Stein, then a Philadelphia Flyers lawyer, argued that Flyers' players shouldn't be loaned to the tournament to play for Team Canada. Their participation was prohibited by the players' own contracts, and why should the NHL owners risk injury to their principal assets just because the Canadian government supported a tournament promoted by Alan Eagleson? It was then, Eagleson writes, that Bill Wirtz came to his rescue:

> Suddenly Bill Wirtz from Chicago stood up and said to Stein, "Gil, you'd better just relax, we need Canada to be dominant. What Alan has done is put the NHL in indirect control of international hockey by his own involvement — meaning we don't have a third party, Hockey Canada, in the driver's seat...Eagleson is one of our partners at the joint-venture level. It is better to have our partner there running it than a stranger."[9]

Once the owners gave him permission to use their players in the tournaments, Eagleson was immediately beholden to them for any gains he received

---

[9]Alan Eagleson, *Power Play: Memoirs of A Hockey Czar*, McClelland & Stewart Inc., Toronto, 1991, p. 152-153.

from the running of the tournaments. As Eagleson reaped the benefits of the tournaments, the owners reaped the benefits of having the chief negotiator for their employees in their back pockets. This came in quite handy during collective bargaining agreements and salary negotiations, as well as during the infamous merger between the World Hockey Association and the NHL. As one anonymous NHL general manager put it: "Al delivers us the players and we give him international hockey. It's that simple."[10]

Eagleson quickly persuaded the players, to whom he was a fiduciary and over whom he exerted total control, to play in the tournaments for little or no pay by telling them that their share of tournament profits would go into their NHL pension fund. But as it turned out, this was a lie: the players' pension did not benefit from the tournaments. Though a small portion of the profits earned by the players went into their pension fund, the contributions did nothing to *increase* their NHL pensions overall. Instead, they merely offset contributions that the owners would have legally been required to make anyway. Of course, the players would have had no way of knowing this because Eagleson had previously agreed to remove player representatives from the pension board.[11]

Between 1972 and 1991, several hundred international games were played as part of these tournaments, including the legendary 1972 Summit Series and five Canada Cup tournaments. Eagleson exercised total control over the operations of the international tournaments, running them as profit-generating businesses and earning substantial revenues. It was in this position that Eagleson enriched himself with large portions of money generated by the tournaments. This included hundreds of thousands of dollars from kickbacks from the sales of Canada Cup advertising; overpayment of salaries and expenses to himself and his associates; and illegal conversion of advertising money into hundreds of thousands of dollars worth of Air Canada passes. All of these schemes reduced the net proceeds to be divided between the NHLPA and the NHL, but the NHL owners simply looked the other way, permitting Eagleson unsupervised, unconstrained control of the tournaments, with the clear understanding that they would receive favors in return.

The investigations done in the United States and Canada also revealed that Eagleson established numerous phony business entities to act as fronts for his wheeling and dealing. Using these corporate subterfuges, Eagleson then funneled payments to himself or his law firm in the form of "legal

---

[10]John Papanek and Bill Brubaker, "The Man Who Rules Hockey," *Sports Illustrated*, July 2, 1984, Pg. 60.

[11]See *Game Misconduct* at 18-42.

fees" or through payments to companies owned by his family. During this same period, Eagleson repeatedly lied to the players, telling them again and again that he did not make a single penny from the international tournaments. In a March 1989 letter sent to every member of the NHLPA, Eagleson wrote:

> I have never received any direct or indirect benefit from international hockey. Neither I, nor any member of my family, nor any company with which I am associated has ever received money directly or indirectly from any international hockey event.[12]

In late 1988, over one hundred NHL players, dissatisfied with Eagleson's performance as NHLPA director, asked Ed Garvey, a private attorney in Madison, Wisconsin, who had formerly been head of the NFL player's association, to evaluate the NHLPA under Eagleson's stewardship. In a 55-page report, dated June 3, 1989, entitled "Confidential Report to the NHLPA Players" (now known as the "Garvey Report"), Garvey wrote forcefully of Eagleson's conflicts:

> Alan wants to head international hockey. He can only do so if the NHL owners and Ziegler agree. Therefore, he must not do things at the bargaining table to antagonize them too much or they will dump him — simple as that.[13]

The report also noted that under Eagleson's leadership "no benefits of any significance were achieved in the entire decade of the 80s through collective bargaining."[14]

As a result of Eagleson's conflicts of interests, along with Eagleson and Wirtz's collusion, on November 7, 1995, five former NHL players filed a class-action suit against Eagleson, Wirtz, John Ziegler, and the 22 teams in existence while Eagleson ran the players' union. The gist of the lawsuit is that the owners colluded with Eagleson to betray the players in the collective bargaining negotiations, violating both the Labor-Management Relations Act (Taft-Hartley) and the Racketeer Influenced and Corrupt Organizations Act (RICO). The charge is that NHL management bribed Eagleson to sell out the players, thus suppressing players' salaries and union benefits for years. As Marty Oberman, the Chicago lawyer who represents the players in the lawsuit, explained, "The scams undertaken by Eagleson could not have taken

---

[12]Copy of letter in author's possession.
[13]Garvey Report at 51. Copy of Garvey Report in author's possession.
[14]*Id.* at 55.

place without the willing connivance of Ziegler and Wirtz. In return for the owners' largess to Eagleson, there was a *quid pro quo*. The *quid pro quo* here was Eagleson's cooperation in labor negotiations. Simply put, they — Wirtz and Ziegler — handed over unsupervised control of international tournament revenues to Eagleson for sweetheart labor deals."[15]

THE GIFT OF GIVING

And it is certainly clear that Wirtz and the rest of the NHL owners received their fair share of benefits by allowing Eagleson to have control over international hockey. In 1982, Eagleson brokered a collective bargaining agreement that even Toronto Maple Leafs president Harold Ballard called a "joke" on the players.[16] Player agent Gus Badali, whose clients included Wayne Gretzky, said that "a couple" of NHL general managers told him point blank that the collective bargaining agreement was the best ever for management. "They certainly don't hide their glee," Badali is quoted as saying.[17] Certainly Harold Ballard didn't. "How do the owners feel about Eagleson?" he said. "We like him....Sure, it's a great contract — for us."[18]

In 1979, during the merger between the NHL and the rival World Hockey Association, Eagleson again stepped up to the plate for the owners. After seven years of battling the rival league, the NHL owners were eager for a merger, if only to stop the bleeding from the bidding wars that had inflated players' salaries. The players, in contrast, were lukewarm to a merger. In exchange for a merger, they wanted to be accorded real free agency, which was the same deal the NBA had agreed upon just a few years earlier after the 1976 NBA-ABA merger. But Eagleson, acting like a *de facto* representative of the owners, told the players that several NHL teams were in a perilous financial state and cautioned the players that the league would not be able to withstand a legal battle over the question whether to grant the players free agency. Through intimidation and lies, Eagleson convinced the players to accept the merger without *any* demands for free agency and with only limited commitments from the owners to increase benefits. With Eagleson doing their bidding, the owners essentially robbed the players blind. As former New York Ranger Brad Park said, "[Eagleson] gave up a competitive situation. And for what? We got nothing in return."[19]

Thanks to Eagleson's assistance, the NHL owners were also able to

[15]Personal conversation between Marty Oberman and author on October 4, 2000.
[16]John Papanek and Bill Brubaker, *Sports Illustrated* at 62.
[17]*Id.*
[18]*Id.*
[19]John Anderson, *The American Lawyer* at 65.

exploit the NHL pension fund for years. In 1990, players like Gordie Howe, with 33 years of service to the NHL, were collecting less than $15,000 (Cdn.) in annual pension. Similarly, Carl Brewer, a four-time all-star with the Maple Leafs, was receiving about $8,000 (Cdn). In 1991, Brewer, Howe, and former NY Ranger Andy Bathgate filed suit against the NHL and recovered a $75 million judgment against the league. It turned out the NHL owners, through their representatives on the pension board, had appropriated the players' pension money for their own uses. And it had been Eagleson, as head of the NHLPA, who had agreed with the NHL owners' request to drop players representation on the pension board, thus opening the door for the owners to act without any player oversight of their own money. "This was our retirement money, and Alan Eagleson had given control over it to the NHL," says Brewer. "Can you believe it?"[20]

Eagleson also agreed to the lack of free agency and acquiesced to nondisclosure of player salaries. It wasn't until Bob Goodenow became the executive director of the NHLPA in 1992 that the union made individual players' salaries public. The NHLPA was the last of the four major professional sports' unions to do so. Keeping player salaries secret was a tremendous advantage to the owners, since without comparable salary information it was difficult for players and agents to gauge their fair market value. Not coincidentally, during the time Eagleson was in charge of the players' association, NHL salaries increased at a percentage far below that of other major professional sports.[21]

Indeed, it was Eagleson's inability to bargain vigorously and effectively on the players' behalf that prompted Ed Garvey to tell Eagleson in a 1989 letter:

> You and [NHL President] Ziegler have become co-commissioners or co-presidents of international hockey as well as the NHL. You have moved into a conflict position that is so deep it would be nearly impossible to untangle you, your relationship with Ziegler and Wirtz, your involvement with international Hockey and your supposed role as leader of the union.[22]

And similarly, in his 1989 Report commissioned by the players, Garvey

---

[20]*Id.*

[21]John Papanek and Bill Brubaker, *Sports Illustrated* at 65. It is not just that average NHL salaries were less than average salaries in professional football, baseball, and basketball. That can be explained due to less money in the sport overall. Under Eagleson's leadership, NHL players' salaries *as a percentage of the owners' overall gross revenues* was also significantly less than in the other professional sports.

[22]*David S. Forbes, et al. v. R. Alan Eagleson, et al.*, 19 F. Supp. 2d 352, 367, 370, August 27, 1998.

concluded in no uncertain terms:

> Alan Eagleson has been a vital part of the NHL establish-
> ment. He has contributed greatly to keeping salaries down,
> profits up. He has helped maintain monopoly status, he
> keeps players tied up, he allows the League to control
> through non-impartial arbitration; he eliminates freedom
> whenever it raises its head; and he keeps you in the dark
> about the economics of the League while singing man-
> agement's song about the 'fragile' NHL.[23]

A GOOD OLD-FASHIONED COVER-UP

Alan Eagleson repeatedly stonewalled the players' efforts to get information about the proceeds from international hockey. As Ed Garvey wrote,
"[The players had] virtually no ability to get detailed information about the
operations of their union, their pension, International Hockey, decision making in the NHL, salaries, the economics of the NHL or any other important
matter impacting their careers."[24] But what is not nearly as well known is that
the NHL owners facilitated Eagleson in hiding his criminal activity.

The international tournaments were a joint venture between the NHL and
the NHLPA, meaning the two entities were to share all the proceeds from the
tournaments. By virtue of the international tournaments being a joint venture,
the owners stood in a fiduciary relationship to the players. This relationship
gave rise to a legal duty on the part of the owners to provide to the players an
honest and accurate accounting of the joint venture's financial matters. But,
as detailed in the NHL players' lawsuit, the NHL owners joined Eagleson in
stonewalling and using intimidation tactics to prevent the players from gath-
ering information about Eagleson's illegal activities.

For example, on January 24, 1991, several retired NHL players, including
Gordie Howe and Bobby Hull, who had been rebuffed previously by
Eagleson, wrote a letter to NHL President John Ziegler requesting a meeting.[25]
They wanted "financial disclosures as to the gross proceeds from interna-

---

[23]Garvey Report at 50.

[24]*Id.*at 2. In his report, Garvey emphasized the audaciousness of Eagleson's non-dis-
closures by noting that Eagleson failed to provide the players "information that is required
by law to be made available to all union members." *Id.*

[25]It should be mentioned that Eagleson only served one-third of his 18-month prison
sentence behind bars before receiving parole, prompting numerous outraged responses
from his victims, including Hull, who said: "There's no justice. That guy should have been

tional hockey from 1972 to date, or any related expenditures." The request was refused. Similarly, on February 25, 1991, ex-NHLer Dave Forbes, the lead plaintiff in the class-action lawsuit by the NHL players, asked Eagleson for a meeting with Ziegler and Ken Sawyer, the NHL treasurer and vice president of finance. Sawyer responded to the letter saying: "You should direct this question to the NHLPA," but he did so knowing full well that Eagleson had already refused all requests from the players and that there was no chance he would comply.

Nevertheless, on March 14, 1991, Forbes again sent specific questions to the NHLPA, including: "Could you provide me with the audited financial statements from all international hockey from 1984?" and "Inform me as to the flow of these funds from international hockey to the NHLPA." He was refused. Then, in April 1991, Forbes again exchanged letters with the NHL's treasurer, Sawyer, who again failed to provide any relevant information.

In addition to the requests by various players for information, Ed Garvey, on behalf of the players, was also rebuffed in his efforts to obtain information from the NHL about international hockey. Furthermore, the NHL encouraged individual team owners to prevent Garvey from meeting with the players at their practice facilities. In addition, NHL President John Ziegler went so far as to bolster Eagleson's position in the union by publicly attacking Garvey. In a speech in Toronto in April 1989, Ziegler said:

> Just look at Mr. Garvey with his football association when he was leading them to two strikes, it cost those players in salaries they will never get back more than 100 million dollars. That's what confrontation does at the bargaining table.[26]

At the same time, Ziegler corroborated Eagleson's false claims that, under Eagleson, the players' union had obtained the best salary levels possible. Ziegler falsely stated: "the National Hockey League player, from a security standpoint, [is] one of the best provided-for players in any professional sport."[27] And he reaffirmed prior false statements made by Eagleson that all the profits from international hockey went into the players' pension fund:

---

pitched in the cell and the key thrown away. I don't know who allowed him to walk, but all he got was a slap on the wrist." Tom Godfrey, "Eagle Out After 6 Months," *The Toronto Sun*, July 8, 1998, Sports, p. 5.

[26]Transcript of Speech by John Ziegler to the Empire Club of Canada, April 6, 1989. Copy in author's possession.

[27]*Id.* at 9.

Our players are entrepreneurs. They are, for example, joint venturers in international hockey. Profits from international hockey are divided 50 percent to the players and 50 percent to the owners. *All of the profits go into the player pensions.* Not only regular pension, but also supplemental pension. This partnership has produced for players more than $10 million dollars of the last eleven year and we expect it will continue to produce at an ever increasing rate.[28] (Emphasis added).

Ziegler also defended Eagleson against criticism that he wasn't a sufficiently zealous negotiator of the players' interests, noting that just because Eagleson was close friends with Wirtz and Ziegler, it didn't mean he wasn't a vigorous spokesmen for the players:

One thing I think you'll find in very inexperienced lawyers, they don't understand that you can advocate to the fullest to give your client absolutely the best he can get, fight the other lawyer tooth and nail and yet, when court adjourns, have dinner and a drink with him and not interfere with your performance. Alan and I were both raised as lawyers in the courtroom. The idea that we can be absolute adversaries and still have a friendship was well-established long ago.[29]

Wirtz also joined in the fun of pumping up and defending Eagleson by announcing, "I think Alan is a brilliant negotiator."[30]

Wirtz and Ziegler's claims that Eagleson was an effective advocate for the players are laughable. In his 1997 book, *Power Plays*, Gil Stein, the former interim President of the NHL, made it clear, with truly astonishing honesty, that the collective bargaining sessions under Eagleson's rule were "a charade of sorts."[31] Stein details how the collective bargaining sessions were "staged" by Eagleson and the NHL power brokers in a "duplicitous manner."[32] As part of the charade put on by Eagleson, Ziegler, and Wirtz, Stein reports that Eagleson would ridicule Ziegler's and Wirtz's proposals in front of the players, not out of any sincere belief in what he was saying, but

[28]*Id.* at 10-11.

[29]Dan Barnes, "Heeeere's Johnny," *The Edmonton Sun*, April 16, 1989, Sports, p. 8.

[30]John Papanek and Bill Brubaker, *Sports Illustrated* at 65.

[31]Gil Stein, *Power Plays: An Inside Look at the Big Business of the National Hockey League*, Carol Publishing Group, Toronto, 1997, p. 100.

[32]*Id.* at 98-101.

because "it looked good in front of the players for Eagleson to tell off the owners."[33] Stein says the negotiations were a theatrical exercise to, as he put it, "[keep] the citizenry pacified."[34] And the most amazing thing, says Stein, was that while it was well known to the owners that these sessions were a fraud, "To us, it appeared the players never suspected the scenario might have been carefully scripted in advance."[35]

How tethered were Eagleson, Wirtz, and Ziegler? How invested were Wirtz and Ziegler in keeping Eagleson head of the union? How much did the NHL benefit from Eagleson's unwillingness to challenge the owners' power? In his book, Stein reveals for the first time that Wirtz and Ziegler worked behind the scenes with Eagleson in 1992 in hopes of overthrowing Bob Goodenow and reinstalling Eagleson as head of the NHLPA. During 1991, when Bob Goodenow was hired to become the new NHLPA executive director, Stein reports that the three amigos — Eagleson, Ziegler and Wirtz — conspired to undermine Goodenow in his upcoming negotiations with the NHL by fomenting a movement among the players for Eagleson's return as executive director. The hope was that by making Goodenow look bad, the players would return to the deposed Eagleson. Stein offers detailed instances of what he calls "the Ziegler-Wirtz plan to embarrass" Goodenow, but the smear campaign backfired and Goodenow was able to use Wirtz and Ziegler's tactics to "unify the union's Executives behind him and to make the players more militant in their stance towards the NHL."[36]

SAVED BY THE STATUTE OF LIMITATIONS — #692

On September 10, 1999, the players' class-action lawsuit was dismissed due to the RICO law's four-year statute of limitations.[37] The case had been filed on Nov. 7, 1995, but Judge Thomas O'Neill, Jr. ruled that the NHL players had knowledge of the alleged collusion between Eagleson and NHL management well before Nov. 7, 1991, making the filing of their lawsuit untimely. In his rulings, the judge made it clear that the case was not dismissed due to a lack of merit and that there was nothing farfetched about the substance of the players' charges. Indeed, the evidence of potential criminal activity by

---

[33]*Id.* at 100.

[34]*Id.*

[35]*Id.* at 101.

[36]*Id.* at 106-107.

[37]*David S. Forbes, et al. v. R. Alan Eagleson, et al.,* Civil Action No. 95-7021, United States District Court for the Eastern District of Pennsylvania, 1999 U.S. Dist. Lexis 13946 (September 10, 1999).

Eagleson and the owners was so overwhelming that the players should have sued Wirtz and Ziegler long before November of 1995.[38] In a tacit admission of the owners' illicit bribes to Eagleson, Judge O'Neill concluded, "No reasonable observer could have concluded that the payments Eagleson was reported to have received were...legitimate."[39] Nevertheless, because the players knew or should have known on or before November 1991 of the crimes being perpetrated against them, the case was dismissed.

Thus, by a legal technicality, it appears that Wirtz will once again escape any *legal* punishment for his actions.[40] But according to Wirtz's defenders, this is how it should be. They argue that even assuming the players' accusations are all true, Wirtz still did nothing wrong. It was, after all, Eagleson who sold-out the players; Wirtz just took advantage of Eagleson's venality. Unlike Eagleson, Wirtz did not have a legal responsibility to protect the players' interests. But this casual dismissal of Wirtz's dealings is difficult to swallow. Large-scale bribery is not something to be whistled away. Legal or not, a briber is a professional seducer. This incident is yet another example of Wirtz using reprehensible tactics to gain a business advantage. His actions are also blatantly hypocritical. In his public statements, Wirtz speaks of his love for the NHL players, going so far as to compare the affections he has for NHL players to the affections he has for his own sons.[41] One can't help but wonder how rigging the labor negotiations and selling-out the players shows the least bit of affection and respect for his beloved players?

---

[38]*David S. Forbes, et al. v. R. Alan Eagleson et al.*, 19 F. Supp. 2d 352, 370-371, August 27, 1998. "These facts were more than sufficient to provide plaintiffs with notice that the NHL defendants might be turning a blind eye to Eagleson's use of international hockey and NHL disability insurance funds to enrich himself." *Id.* at 371. "That they [the NHL players] may not have recognized that these facts added up to unlawful bribes is irrelevant." *Id.* at 372.

[39]*Id.* at 372.

[40]The plaintiffs appealed the lower court's dismissal of the case, but on October 18, 2000, they lost their appeal. See *Forbes v. Eagleson et al,* No. 99-1803, 2000 U.S. App. Lexis 25918, United States Court of Appeals for the Third Circuit, October 17, 2000. It is uncertain at this time whether plaintiffs will appeal to the U.S. Supreme Court.

[41]Of the NHL players who partook in the 1998 Olympics on behalf of the United States, Wirtz said: "These young men are not only a credit to the NHL, but also to their country. In fact, I would be proud to be their father, and my sons would love to have them as their brothers." Tim Sassone, "Hawks Owner Wirtz Defends U.S. Hockey Players In Letter," *Chicago Daily Herald*, March 13, 1998, Sports, p. 4.

"I'm fed up with people attacking my integrity.
It's an outrage! How dare they imply I have integrity!"

Chapter 7

Abuse of Power
As Owner of the Blackhawks

*"Decency consists not in never stealing or lying,
but in having the good sense to know
when to stop stealing and lying."*

— *Fran Lebowitz*

Since Bill Wirtz took control of the Backhawks in 1966, the Chicago sports media and Blackhawks' fans have shown him little more than contempt (and *vice versa*). "This is a man," the *Chicago Daily Herald's* Tim Sassone has written, "who just isn't convincing about his desire to win a Stanley Cup."[1] Sassone has asked in vain why the Blackhawks can't have "an owner who is committed to winning championships…an owner who is up to date in his thinking and not stuck in 1966?"[2] *Sun-Times'* reporter Herb Gould has written that the Blackhawks are a franchise that "counts its championships at the bank, not on the ice."[3] Fellow *Sun-Times'* columnist Jay Mariotti has complained: "In a town of contemptible sports owners, [Wirtz] has emerged as the biggest villain of all, a man who repeatedly sabotages the popularity and high hopes of his franchise in deference to the almighty dollar."[4] The *Daily Herald's* Barry Rozner has sarcasti-

[1]Tim Sassone, "Blackhawks Only Have Themselves To Blame for Debacle," *Chicago Daily Herald*, August 24, 1997, Sports, p. 2.

[2]Tim Sassone, "Wirtz Blew it With Hull…So What Else Is New?" *Chicago Daily Herald*, July 5, 1998, Sports, p. 3.

[3]Herb Gould, "Deal Further Damages Hockey In Chicago," *Chicago Sun-Times*, August 18, 1996, Sports, p. 21.

[4]Jay Mariotti "Wirtz Doesn't Have Gumption To Go for Cup," *Chicago Sun-Times*, March 4, 1996, Sports, p. 90.

cally remarked, "Bill Wirtz would rather have his spleen removed with a bottle opener than give back a dime,"[5] adding that "Someone told Bill Wirtz his team had quit on him and the Blackhawks' owner was thrilled. Apparently, he thought that meant he wouldn't have to pay them for the rest of this season."[6] Ex-*Tribune* sports columnist Bernie Lincicome has observed that Wirtz "[operates] his team as if the players ought to pay him for the honor of wearing 'that Indianhead' on their shirts."[7] Lincicome once even compared Wirtz unfavorably to Adolph Hitler. In reference to sympathetic remarks Bobby Hull reportedly made about Adolph Hitler to a Moscow newspaper (remarks later denied by Hull), Lincicome wrote: "In his rebuttal, Hull identifies Hitler as 'the most evil and despicable person who ever lived,' and remember, Hull played for Bill Wirtz."[8]

Wirtz and his lackeys like to explain away the public condemnation by arguing that Wirtz is just the victim of unfair media attacks. Their mantra is that all sports team owners are hated and that there's nothing any owner can do about it. As Wirtz puts it, owners are born to be hated: "Club presidents aren't in the business of being loved by fans. Anytime you raise prices, you are unpopular. I guess if you want to go broke, you can be popular."[9] There is, of course, a patina of truth to this — owners are often the victim of unfair attacks. But, as the facts below reveal, Bill Wirtz is not the innocent victim he and his hucksters make him out to be — far from it indeed.

As one of the great storied teams in NHL history, the Blackhawks have enjoyed every advantage any sports owner could possibly desire — loyal fans, incredible wealth, enormous profitability (not to mention the greatest

[5]Barry Rozner, "What's This? Wolves Make Money-Back Guarantee," *Chicago Daily Herald*, April 16, 1998, Sports, p. 1.

[6]Barry Rozner, "Gray's Badgering Works in Rose's Favor," *Chicago Daily Herald*, October 26, 1999, Sports, p. 1.

[7]Bernie Lincicome, "4th Time No Charm For Pulford," *Chicago Tribune*, December 3, 1999, p. 1N.

[8]Bernie Lincicome, "You Expected Great Insight From A Hockey Player?" *Chicago Tribune*, August 27, 1998, p. 1N.

[9]Mike Kiley, "NHL Owners Love Wirtz — Even If Hawks Fans Don't," *Chicago Tribune*, January 18, 1991, p. 3C. Exculpatory remarks are a constant refrain from Wirtz and his cronies. Examples include: (1) Wirtz: "I think everyone wants to be loved. But you don't want to be broke, either. And I learned early that if you want to be liked by the public, don't get into this business." Lisa Twyman Bessone, "Power Play," *Chicago Magazine*, January 1992, p. 91; (2) Wirtz: "And why should you be loved? You raise ticket prices, you raise beer prices, you raise prices of the soda, hot dogs and the parking. It's always the 'damn owners' fault." Brian Hanley, "The Word from Wirtz," *Chicago Sun-Times*, January 15, 1995, p. 23; (3) Wirtz: "If you don't win the Stanley Cup every year, of course you're going to be criti-

logo in professional sports). At the very least, Wirtz's tenure as owner inspires ingratitude merely for not being great. But instead of greatness, the team has wallowed in mediocrity. The team currently owns the longest drought without a Stanley Cup in the NHL — 40 years and counting. During Wirtz's tenure, every other original six team — Boston, Detroit, Montreal, New York Rangers, and Toronto — has won the Cup at least once. And today, entering the year 2001, the Blackhawks are regarded as little better than an expansion team. But while the glaring absence of any Stanley Cup banners is a shame, it is not Wirtz's real crime. His real crime as owner is that he has engaged in the systematic abuse of his steady customers over the course of the last 35 years. His various abuses can be divided into four distinct categories: unadulterated greed; lying to the fans; mismanagement; and civic irresponsibility.

PROFITS ÜBER ALLES

It is impossible to name another hockey owner who has cashed in less on the ice and more off the ice than Bill Wirtz. Wirtz has combined on-ice futility with off-ice profitability in a manner surpassing any other NHL owner in history. The record is clear that, rather than operating his team with a focussed commitment to building a winner, Wirtz has primarily used the Blackhawks as a vehicle to foster his personal wealth. "Wirtz is a hard-nosed businessman who never loses sight of the bottom line," admits Gil Stein, former NHL commissioner.[10] Stein tells a story about how he and Wirtz and Philadelphia Flyers owner Ed Snider were all standing together prior to the start of the 1992 All-Star Game in Philadelphia. Snyder had just been booed on the ice by a number of fans. "I hate when they boo me," said Snyder. "Don't let it bother you, Eddie," Wirtz laughed, "just do what I do. Every time Chicago fans boo me, I raise their ticket prices."[11] A joke to be sure, but it's one that corresponds with too much reality to be dismissed merely as a joke. Fact is, Bill Wirtz himself makes no effort to hide his lust for money, boasting that he

---

cized." Deposition testimony of Bill Wirtz in *Mark G. Weinberg and Blue Line Publishing, Inc. v. Chicago Blackhawks Hockey Team, Inc.*, case No. 96-L-1099, Circuit Court of Cook County, Law Division, p. 81, lines 22-23; (4) Bob Pulford: "I think anyone in management, regardless of the sport, there are few of us that are loved. Like Jerry Krause. He won the world championship six times. He's brilliant and he's booed. So maybe it goes with the territory." Mike Kiley, "Who is the Real Bob Pulford?" *Chicago Sun-Times*, December 09, 1999, p. 152.

[10]Gil Stein, *Power Plays: An Inside Look at The Big Business of The National Hockey League*, A Birch Lane Press Book, Secaucus, N.J., 1997, p. 42.

[11]*Id.*

considers his nickname "Dollar Bill" a high compliment to his business acumen,[12] conveniently choosing to ignore that the nickname is the public's way to certify Wirtz's repute for unyielding predation.

The proof of Wirtz's profiteering is in the numbers. The Blackhawks are annually among the most lucrative NHL franchises. According to data from *Financial World* magazine, no team is even close to the Blackhawks in terms of profitability.[13] The numbers show that in 1997 the Blackhawks were *the* most profitable team in the league by an enormous margin, earning $26.9 million, $9 million more than the league's next most profitable team. The other big-market teams — the Detroit Red Wings, the Philadelphia Flyers, and the Toronto Maple Leafs — are not even close to the Blackhawks when it comes to turning a profit. By way of comparison, the Red Wings, who won the Stanley Cup in 1997 and had 20 playoff games' worth of extra profits, still earned $17 million *less* than the Blackhawks, who had just six playoff games, losing to Colorado in the first round.

But the most eye-popping number isn't the Blackhawks' incredible profitability; it's a number not even on the chart but one that must be calculated separately. It is the percentage of total revenue to player salaries. The chart reveals that in 1997 the Blackhawks spent $23.8 million on player salaries and had revenue of $73.1 million for a percentage of player salaries to revenue of 32.5 percent, the lowest in the league. The Bruins were next lowest at 34.2 percent, and no other team in the league was under 40 percent. The league average is 51 percent. By way of comparison, in the NBA, 55 percent of the gross revenue goes to the players under their latest collective bargaining agreement. In other words, as a percentage of overall revenue, Wirtz spent less money on players' salaries than any other NHL or NBA owner.

The Blackhawks defend themselves by saying that their player payroll is annually in the top-third of the league. Peter Wirtz, the team's vice-president of marketing and the heir apparent to the Blackhawks' throne, takes umbrage

[12]Deposition testimony of Bill Wirtz in *Mark G. Weinberg and Blue Line Publishing, Inc. v. Chicago Blackhawks Hockey Team, Inc.*, case No. 96-L-1099, Circuit Court of Cook County, Law Division, p. 57, lines 2-13. Copy in possession of author.

[13]The *Financial World* numbers are from 1997 and are based on three years' of preceding revenues. Since Wirtz and other NHL owners refuse to open their books, these numbers are the most accurate figures publicly available. The numbers change from year to year due to attendance fluctuations, but if anything the numbers underreport actual profits, as it is well known that the owners are able to play numerous accounting games to hide their teams' profitability. *Financial World* was published for 95 years, from 1902 until 1997, but ceased publication in 1998. Hence, this was the last year for which these profit figures are available.Kurt Badenhausen and Christopher Nikolov, "Sports Valuations—More Than A Game," *Financial World*, June 17, 1997, p. 40.

NHL FRANCHISE VALUES FROM JUNE 1997 *FINANCIAL WORLD*

	Gate Receipts[1]	Media Revenues[2]	Venue Revenues[3]	Total Revenues[4]	Player Costs[5]	Operating Expenses[6]	Operating Income[7]	Franchise Value[8]
1. Blackhawks	$38.7	$6.0	$24.5	$73.1	$23.8	$46.3	$26.9	$151
2. Rangers	36.0	8.3	20.7	70.4	34.1	60.1	10.2	147
3. Red Wings	37.5	8.3	15.0	65.2	30.6	56.1	9.1	146
4. Bruins	35.9	11.8	12.8	64.9	22.2	47.2	17.8	130
5. Flyers	34.1	7.9	8.7	53.6	22.4	43.9	9.7	128
6. Maple Leafs	24.7	8.4	8.8	46.2	23.4	42.9	3.4	105
7. Mighty Ducks	22.6	5.5	9.0	39.5	15.8	32.5	6.9	104
8. Sharks	25.5	4.2	10.5	42.4	18.9	34.4	8.1	104
9. Penguins	35.6	7.0	4.6	48.6	24.2	38.5	10.1	96
10. Blues	38.1	5.2	8.6	54.8	28.5	48.5	6.3	95
11. Canadiens	22.7	7.2	6.4	40.2	20.1	40.6	-0.4	95
12. Canucks	26.3	7.3	4.8	42.7	26.5	43.0	-0.3	91
13. Capitals	22.1	4.7	7.3	36.5	18.5	36.0	0.5	85
14. Kings	27.8	7.0	4.8	40.4	28.4	42.4	-2.0	83
15. Avalanche	25.9	3.0	6.6	36.9	21.5	37.5	-0.6	81
16. Devils	27.1	7.2	8.5	43.6	23.4	39.4	4.3	79
17. Islanders	19.8	10.9	5.0	37.1	18.0	33.2	3.9	74
18. Sabres	19.3	5.1	4.1	29.3	19.9	32.7	-3.3	74
19. Flames	22.3	5.0	8.4	38.6	17.1	30.8	7.8	72
20. Senators	17.7	5.5	6.4	31.9	13.8	31.8	0.1	67
21. Panthers	23.2	5.4	2.7	32.6	17.8	33.5	-0.9	67
22. Lightning	12.9	5.5	5.7	25.0	15.4	29.1	-4.2	64
23. Stars	26.9	4.3	1.9	33.9	21.4	34.9	-1.0	63
24. Oilers	13.7	5.0	6.1	27.6	11.7	27.7	-0.1	52
25. Whalers	16.6	4.1	2.2	23.8	22.4	32.9	-9.2	48
26. Coyotes	11.9	4.6	3.3	20.6	22.8	32.3	-11.7	43
League Averages	25.6	6.3	8.0	42.3	21.6	38.8	3.5	90

Note: All amounts are in millions of dollars. Except for franchise value, all figures are for 1995-1996 season. 1. Gross gate receipts, including club seats, but excluding sales taxes. 2. Includes national TV, local TV, cable TV, satellite TV and radio. 3. Includes suite rentals and tickets, concessions, parking, venue advertising and naming rights. 4. Includes revenues not shown in table, such as licensing and merchandise. 5. Includes salaries, deferred payments, bonuses, insurance, workers compensation and pensions. 6. Includes player costs, travel, marketing, administrative, media and venue expenses. 7. Total revenues less operating expenses. 8. Based on the last three years average total revenues, venue situation and revenue and financial prospects for the next two years.

Source: *Financial World,* June 17, 1997

at the suggestion that his father is more interested in turning a profit than winning a Cup. "Our payroll is regularly among the top one-third in the league," Peter insists. "It really bothers me when people say my father doesn't care about winning or that he isn't willing to spend the money."[14] Peter's assertion is correct — the Blackhawks' payroll *is* routinely in the top-third of the league. And this puts them in the same spending category as teams like the Anaheim Mighty Ducks and the New Jersey Devils, who earn profits of $3-to-$4 million a year (see chart). But the Blackhawks earn as much as 700 percent more than that in profits! The we-are-in-the top-third-of-the-league argument ignores the reality that the Blackhawks' overall profitability is easily and consistently among the top three NHL teams. No one has ever argued that the Blackhawks don't spend *any* money on players, only that the spread between their profitability and players' salaries is larger than any other team's and that Wirtz has preferred to pocket that spread for himself rather than plow it back into the team to build a champion.

But beyond the hard numbers, the proof of Wirtz's greed can also be found in the lost talents and angry attacks of former Blackhawks' players. It is safe to say that no team in the NHL has lost as many players due to money disputes as the Hawks. The list is a long one — Bobby Hull, Jeremy Roenick, Eddie Belfour, Bernie Nicholls, and Joe Murphy, among others. Wirtz's one major instance of signing a high-priced free-agent, Doug Gilmour, to a three-year, $18-million dollar contract in 1998, which was a huge flop that ended in Gilmour being traded after two seasons to Buffalo for a warm body named Michal Grosek (who himself was then soon shipped off to the New York Rangers), doesn't undo and can't paper over a lifetime of running away from spending money. Over the years, several ex-Blackhawk players have called Wirtz on his lack of commitment to winning, an unusual and risky occurrence in any professional sport, since players never know where they may end up playing and burning bridges is never a smart career move. There are numerous examples, but the charge of former Hawks center Bernie Nicholls is typical enough: "If they wanted to win, they could win there. The Blackhawks have as much money or more than any team in the league. But as long as they're competitive...that's going to be good enough for management. And because of that, I feel bad for the fans. They're great fans, and they've been through it all. They deserve better."[15]

[14]Bob Kravitz, "Blackholes: Chicago Ignores Blackhawks," *ESPN The Magazine*, November 13, 2000, p. 110.

[15]Brian Hanley, "Power Play: Roenick Not Worth It; Nicholls Also Learned Complaints Don't Pay," *Chicago Sun-Times*, August 18, 1996, p. 20. Other players' comments include the following: Eddie Belfour, traded after money squabbles with the Hawks to the San Jose

Two of the most infamous examples of Wirtz's refusal to spend top dollars on superior talent must be recounted here, in all their painful detail.

Bobby Hull: In 1972, when Bill Wirtz and his father, Arthur, allowed Bobby Hull to sign a million-dollar contract to play for the Winnipeg Jets of the World Hockey Association, it was arguably the worst personnel decision made by a sports team owner in history.[16] The saddest part of it all is that Hull, who had played 14 years in Chicago and had finished the last year of his contract, had made it clear to the Blackhawks that he wanted to stay. "I thought I was always going to be a Blackhawk," he said. "Back then, we stayed with our teams. A player had loyalty to his particular organization. Now, it's all more corporate."[17]

But as Hull describes the events of 1972, the Blackhawks made little effort to try to keep him. Hull was even willing to take less money than Winnipeg was offering to remain a Blackhawk. The negotiations for the 1972 season started in February of 1972. As Hull told Stan Fischler, "The whole thing has made me wonder what the hell they [the Wirtzes] were thinking. They must have thought I was bluffing, or they must have been gambling that the Winnipeg offer would fall through. If anything, I made the Wirtzes' job easier by saying right at the start of all this that I wanted to stay in Chicago

---

Sharks on Jan. 25, 1997, said: "It's always a struggle for money there. When you put money ahead of winning, that's a sad thing. That's not what the game is about." Rich Strom, "Appropriate End To 'A [Blackhawks] Nightmare'," *Chicago Tribune*, April 19, 1998, p. 1N. Jeremy Roenick, traded to Phoenix in August of 1996, condemned the Blackhawks for their unwillingness to commit to paying top dollar for their best players: "When it comes to negotiating contracts they're very tight and very stubborn spending the bucks. This is the '90s, and if you want to have a good team you have to go out and spend the money. It takes money to get quality players." Tim Sassone, "Coyotes Edge Hawks; Roenick Points Finger at Wirtz For Poor Start," *Chicago Daily Herald*, October 14, 1997, Sports, p. 1. Even as nice and mild-mannered a guy as former Hawks goalie Jeff Hackett, who was traded with Eric Weinrich to the Canadiens in November of 1998, has damned the Blackhawks for their stinginess. Commenting on the firing of Dirk Graham as Blackhawks head coach in February of 1999, Hackett said, "It's too bad. I didn't see it coming. It's only been 59 games, he hasn't had a chance. There's more problems there than the coach. A lot of questionable things have happened in the last three years, but Dirk paid the price for some other people's mistakes. It starts way back with when they traded Jeremy. It was all about money." Canadian Press, "Hackett feels for Graham," Tuesday, February 23, 1999, Montreal.

[16]I say 'arguably' and not 'definitely' because the Boston Red Sox' decision to trade Babe Ruth to the Yankees in 1919 may have been worse. But at least the Red Sox got something in return for Ruth — $125,000 in cold cash and a $300,000 loan to Red Sox owner Harry Frazee — whereas the Blackhawks got nothing for Hull.

[17]John Leptich, "Roenick Deal A Mistake? Hull Knows All Too Well," *Chicago Sun-Times*, August 28, 1996, p. 118.

and that I didn't expect them to come close to matching the Winnipeg offer. But they never took any serious steps to offer me a contract until two weeks before I signed with Winnipeg. Not even sit down and talk and start negotiating. If the Wirtzes had made me any kind of offer, that would have given us a starting point to talk, and I'm sure we could have worked something out, and I would have ended up staying in Chicago."[18]

Bill Wirtz insists he and his father did try to negotiate with Hull in good faith, but according to Hull, the Hawks never sent any meaningful signals of trying to keep him and never made a contract offer until the final moments of his departure to Winnipeg: "The day before I was leaving for Winnipeg, the Blackhawks hand delivered me a contract for five years worth $1.25 million. I said, 'It's too late guys. Take this back to Mr. Wirtz and tell him to stuff it.'"[19]

Though Hull was already 33 years old, he still had plenty of good years left. He was a productive player past his 39th birthday. He turned 39 midway through his last full season with the Jets in 1977-78, scoring 46 goals and 117 points in 77 games. In his six full seasons with the Jets, Hull had 301 goals and 633 points in 407 games, averaging 50 goals and 106 points a season. At age 36, in the 1974-75 season, Hull scored a career high 77 goals and 142 points in 78 games. The next season he had 53 goals and 123 points in 80 games. He played only 34 games the following season, but he still had 21 goals and 53 points. Although it can be argued that Hull posted these impressive numbers in the inferior WHA, Hulls insists otherwise: "I never lost it. What I lost was my desire, and then I quit."[20]

Eric Lindros: The second historic instance of Wirtz's penny-pinching blunders occurred in 1992 when Wirtz had the opportunity to obtain manchild Eric Lindros, but once again refused to spend the money. In 1991, the Quebec Nordiques selected Lindros with the first pick in the entry draft, but he refused to play there, so the next year in June during the week of the 1992 entry draft, Nordiques owner Marcel Aubut took bids to trade Lindros. Blackhawks' GM Mike Keenan had worked out a deal to obtain Lindros. The Hawks would have sent Ed Belfour, Steve Larmer, Steve Smith, Dean McAmmond, Karl Dykhuis, a No. 1 draft pick and upwards of $15 million to the Nordiques in exchange for Lindros' signing rights. (Roenick wouldn't have been part of the deal because he signed a contract in 1991 that included a no-trade-to-Quebec clause, a clause that was subsequently ruled to be

---

[18]Stan Fischler, *Slashing*, Thomas Y. Cromwell Company, New York, 1974, p. 108-109.

[19]Dan O'Neill, "No Jet Lag...At Age 50, Bobby Hull Is As Candid As Ever," *St. Louis Post-Dispatch*, April 30, 1989, Sports, p. 12.

[20]Dave Luecking, "Hull Is From Durable Stock, History Shows," *St. Louis Post-Dispatch*, October 5, 1997, Sports, p. 8.

invalid). But Wirtz nixed the deal, because he refused to spend even one penny for Lindros.

"Mr. Wirtz didn't want to spend the money," said Keenan, adding, "I said you had an opportunity to have Jeremy Roenick and Eric Lindros on the same team in Chicago Stadium. I said any money you have to give out now will come back to you. But he couldn't see the vision and didn't want to spend the money."[21] Keenan insists that if Wirtz had any financial foresight the trade would have put the Hawks in a position to be an NHL powerhouse: "We had a trade on the table that was never granted that probably would have put us over the top. That would have given us a tremendous opportunity to make a run at the Cup. The great thing about it was that we would have kept Roenick and Chelios, and we still had Hasek."[22] In a direct slap at Wirtz, Keenan has said, "We were trying to do something that would've shocked everyone. But some people weren't ready for change."[23] Wirtz has never confirmed or denied this incident, but Quebec GM at the time, Pierre Page, has confirmed Keenan's story, saying "Keenan went to him [Wirtz], but he wouldn't pay a nickel."[24]

Finally, proof of Wirtz's money-madness can also be seen in the United Center itself. Built in 1994, the United Center has 216 skyboxes, more skyboxes than any other stadium in the world. Some arenas are built to generate excitement, but the United Center was built to generate revenues. There is nothing inherently wrong with an abundance of skyboxes, but there is something wrong with an owner's willingness to diminish the average fans' enjoyment of the games in exchange for skybox revenues. You don't have to be an architectural critic to know that the triple layer of skyboxes that fill the United Center comes at a huge cost. Nevertheless, Blair Kamin, the *Chicago Tribune*'s architectural critic, spoke for many when he damned the mall-like atmosphere of the United Center for its lousy acoustics: "Even where I was sitting, in a $30 seat near the bottom of the upper deck, you barely could hear the bounce of the ball, the squeak of the players' shoes or the ball rippling through the cords of the net. It was as though the players were swimming in a fish bowl and we fans were simply staring inside."[25] The stadium's immensi-

[21]Viv Bernstein, "Playing to a New York Crowd," *The Hartford Courant*, October 5, 1993, p. D8.

[22]Tim Sassone, "Keenan Laments Missed Deal," *Chicago Daily Herald*, November 23, 1997, Sports, p. 3.

[23]Steve Rosenbloom, "Remember, Hawks Fans: Keenan Wanted Lindros," *Chicago Sun-Times*, April 20, 1995, p. 103.

[24]*Id.*

[25]Blair Kamin, "Don't Take Me Out To The Mall Game," *Chicago Tribune*, February 5, 1995, p. 5C. Kamin's remarks are true for hockey games too, where the swish and swoosh of the players' skating and the noise of the puck and players' sticks is lost in the 300-level.

ty is a direct result of the extra ring of skyboxes above the 300 level that forced the architects to raise the roof so high that the noises of the playing fields and the noises of the fans is lost in the ether. Instead of being trapped and redirected down to the floor, the roar of the crowd disappears into the night. (On the positive side, the United Center's bathrooms do smell nicer than the old Chicago Stadium's.)

The guaranteed revenues generated by corporate skyboxes also raises the question whether Wirtz's already tenuous commitment to winning hasn't been softened even further. Is it a mere coincidence that the Blackhawks have floundered miserably since moving into the United Center? With the five-year skybox deals, owners are now guaranteed their income even before the season's start. As a result, there is less of an incentive than ever before for icing a winning team. Winning will now only make a marginal difference to the overall bottom-line. There was a time when teams were dependent on regular attendance to generate their profits, but now Joe Fan is less important than ever. I remember about 20 years ago when ballplayers started getting big, multi-year contracts, and writers used to complain that "they don't play as hard once they know their money is guaranteed?" There was never any evidence that it was true of players, but it certainly looks as if it may be true of certain owners like Wirtz.

TELL ME LIES, TELL ME SWEET LITTLE LIES

Over the years, Blackhawks' fans have also been subjected to unbearable lies and bullshit from Bill Wirtz. As shown in preceding chapters, Wirtz's testimony under oath has been ridiculed by several courts for its duplicity. But Wirtz has not reserved his lying for only those occasions where he must swear falsely to God. He's proved himself to be quite an adept liar to Joe Fan too. We're not talking about little lies that amount to mere puffery, like the time he compared the young Eric Daze to Maurice "Rocket" Richard. The lies that gnaw are the ones where Wirtz plays the fans for fools, knowingly misrepresenting the facts for the purpose of fattening his own pocketbook. In a way, Wirtz's lying is even more contemptible than his greed. For the lying suggests an arrogant belief that we, the public, are too stupid to see through it all. Somehow, the greed isn't a personal insult to the fans, whereas the lies — hollow lies no less — are an insult to all of our intelligence.

Whopper No. 1 is Wirtz's infamous defense of his no-television policy. The Hawks are the only professional team of the four major sports that refuse to televise any of their home games. Wirtz's public justification for the policy is that he is doing so out of respect and obligation to his loyal season-ticket holders. "I will never sell our season-ticket holders down the river," Wirtz says emphatically.[26] "We are loyal to our season-ticket holders by allowing them to see the home games," he swears.[27] "Our season-reservation holders are first, second and third priority. I never want to compromise their exclusivity," he says resolutely, as his nose and wallet grow bigger and bigger.[28]

Everyone knows that Wirtz's no-television policy has nothing to do with loyalty to his patrons; it is about loyalty to his profits. Even Wirtz's own son, Peter, has admitted that his father's no-television policy is all about generating greater revenues.[29] (Zen koan: Is a lie that no one believes still a lie?) Bill Wirtz's refusal to televise the home games arises not from any concern for his patrons but from the mistaken belief that doing so will result in fewer fans coming to the games. Forget that the evidence over the last 30 years indisputably reveals that in the long run television exposure increases fan interest and attendance. On this one, empirical evidence is not going to persaude Wirtz. Wirtz is haunted by the ghost of his father, Arthur, who despised television and regarded it as the great enemy of large arena owners. Immediately following WWII, it was widely feared that television would ruin the gate receipts of large arenas because consumers would now find their popular entertainment only on television. Indeed, records from the period 1947-1955 show that television was a major factor for a loss in revenue at both Chicago Stadium and Madison Square Garden.[30] 45 years later, Wirtz has remained stuck in his dead father's outdated 1950's mentality that distrusts television. As the *Chicago Tribune*'s Bob Verdi has put it:

> Some of Bill's confidants surmise that, whenever he's in
> doubt, he operates according to what he imagines his dad
> would have done. By extension, Bill might fear that if he
> allows Hawk home games on TV, Arthur not only would roll
> over in his grave, but storm out of it to give his son 10 lash-
> es with a hockey stick.[31]

[26]Lisa Twyman Bessone, "Power Play," *Chicago Magazine*, January, 1992, p. 89.

[27]Mike Kiley, "NHL Owners Love Wirtz — Even If Hawks Fans Don't," *Chicago Tribune*, January 18, 1991, p. 3C.

[28]Robert Markus, "Wirtz Not Fan Favorite - But His Team Sure Is," *Chicago Tribune*, June 1, 1992, p. 1C.

[29]At the Blackhawks first-ever town hall meeting, held July 27, 2000, Peter Wirtz admitted that his father's no-television policy was about generating greater "gate-receipts." Peter also told the Hawks' fans in attendance that the organization was in the process of "evaluating our television policy." Rest assured, no one believed him. See Brian Hanley, "Passionate Fans Want to See the Same Thing from Hawks," *Chicago Sun-Times*, July 28, 2000, p. 129.

[30]See *United States v. International Boxing Club*, 150 F. Supp. 397, 409 (1957).

[31]Bob Verdi, "Dollar Bill Costing Himself Plenty," *Chicago Tribune*, January 11, 1996, p. 1C.

Whopper No. 2 is Wirtz's false dichotomy between profits and the poorhouse. Wirtz routinely suggests that he can't change his skinflint ways or he will go broke. Asked whether the booing by fans bothers him, Wirtz has replied: "I don't mind it. We're the oldest establishment in ice hockey. We have survived. I'd rather be booed and be in business than be loved and be in Chapter 11."[32] Elsewhere, Wirtz has said: "I think everyone wants to be loved. But you don't want to be broke, either."[33] Broke? Chapter 11? Call me crazy, but even if Bill Wirtz showed a little commitment to winning, he'd still have enough money for beer and pretzels. For him, it's wealth or ruin, prince or pauper, billionaire or beggar. There's no middle ground, no in-between, no proportionality. This false, exaggerated dichotomy is merely an act of self-delusion that allows Wirtz to satisfy his unquenchable appetite for profit.

Whopper No. 3 is Wirtz's shedding crocodile tears over the high price of Blackhawks' tickets. Asked by a local reporter what he thought about the cost of tickets, Wirtz replied, "Our ticket prices are god-awful — I mean, $75 for a ticket. Everything had to be increased for the players' salaries."[34] This is a sentiment so false and hypocritical it makes you gnash your teeth. Wirtz has never tempered his own appetite for profits, and yet he has the chutzpah to express sympathy with the fans over the "god-awful" ticket prices! In expressing such monumentally fraudulent sympathy, Wirtz is playing the typical owners' game of blaming the players' salaries for all the ills in professional sports, thereby attempting to align himself in some kind of victimhood with the fans against the oh-so-greedy players. Wirtz's sympathy is as genuine as Keith Magnuson's front teeth.

Whopper No. 4 is the "You can't buy a championship" argument. This line is employed by Wirtz and his underlings to defend against the team's lack of aggressive spending on free-agents. It's true you can't buy a championship. A championship is the result of many factors — good drafting, good trading, a good minor-league system, and good luck. But is there any doubt that the intelligent and aggressive use of money is one element of success in professional sports? The raging debate, after all, in major league baseball revolves around the question whether the Yankees' four World Series championships in five years isn't largely due to their superior financial might. Wirtz, however, has used the you-can't-buy-a-championship argument to avoid spending money that might cut into his sacred bottom-line. As one of

---

[32]Brian Hanley, "The Word from Wirtz," *Chicago Sun-Times*, January 15, 1995, p. 23.
[33]Lisa Twyman Bessone, "Power Play," *Chicago Magazine*, January, 1992, p. 89.
[34]Brian Hanley, "The Word from Wirtz," *Chicago Sun-Times*, January 15, 1995, p. 23.

the wealthiest teams in the NHL, the Hawks have a huge advantage over less financially secure teams. It hardly need be said that the teams that win in the NHL are the ones that use every edge they can to achieve victory. Nevertheless, Wirtz has refused to exploit his team's financial strength. Moreover, as a non-corporate, non-public entity, the Wirtz family is not beholden to shareholders and thus has more financial flexibility to spend money than publicly-owned enterprises like the Rangers, who routinely out-spend the Blackhawks. Unsurprisingly, one of Wirtz's favorite topics in recent years has been to point out how the Rangers can't be having much fun losing with the league's highest payroll.[35]

There have been other memorable lies too, as when Wirtz and Bob Pulford both claimed that Jeremy Roenick would be a Blackhawk for life. (That life apparently be a fruit fly's.) In a meeting just before the All-Star break in 1996, General Manager Bob Pulford calmed any fears that Roenick would be traded. Speaking for the organization, Pulford told Roenick he would be with the Hawks for the rest of his career. (Who knew Pulford was speaking about himself?) As Pulford relayed the message to the public, "We have no intention of trading him, and I said something like that to him. With all the rumors going around, I wanted him to know how we feel about him. He's going to be with us, is all, the way Stan Mikita was with the Chicago organization his whole career. He's a great player like Denis Savard and Mikita were for the club."[36] Six months later Roenick was shaking sand out of his cup in Phoenix.

Before that, there was the bizarre press conference on Nov. 6, 1992, where Wirtz announced that Mike Keenan had "quit" as Blackhawks' GM. Wirtz publicly stated that Keenan left the organization on his own terms, expressing regret over Keenan's decision to resign and calling Keenan's departure "a loss for the Hawks' family."[37] In fact, Keenan was run out of town on a rail by Wirtz. In a power struggle between Keenan and Pulford, Keenan did not want to be subject to Pulford's oversight. Such independence was absolutely unacceptable to Wirtz, who promptly canned Keenan. In defense of Wirtz, Pulford is ever fond of saying that Keenan didn't just want Pulford's job, he wanted Wirtz's job too. This is supposed to be a clever dig at Keenan's power-hunger, but in saying this, Pulford is at least admitting that

[35]Tim Sassone, "Wirtz's Words Not What Hawks fans Needed to Hear," *Chicago Daily Herald*, December 16, 1997, Sports, p. 10.

[36]Mike Kiley, "Roenick A Hawk For Life? Team Promises To Rework His Contract For Next Season," *Chicago Tribune*, February 13, 1994, p. 1.

[37]Blackhawks news conference, Nov. 6, 1992.

Keenan *was* fired, which is more than Wirtz has ever done.

Wirtz's habitual lying has been compounded by a maddening reclusiveness, a reclusiveness that is nothing if not indicative of a haughty detachment
from the fans and their concerns. It's no secret that over the years Wirtz has
become one of the most invisible owners in all of professional sports. The
Daily Herald's Tim Sassone has called Bill Wirtz "smug" in the distance he
keep from the fans and the media, and he has observed that "as far as owners
go, Bill Wirtz is probably the most reclusive in Chicago sports."[38] Wirtz's
absence is so much expected by Hawks' fans that there wasn't even the tiniest
bit of surprise when Wirtz was a no-show at the first-ever Blackhawks' town-
hall meeting, on July 27, 2000, a forum for only the most loyal fans. In his
place, the indifferent Wirtz sent his son, Peter, who does not seem to share his
father's disdain for the fans. Grateful for the smallest sign of attentiveness
from the Wirtz family, the 550 fans at the meeting expressed near-fawning
appreciation and gratitude to young Wirtz for attending the event and subject-
ing himself to their questions and concerns.

HEY! SOME OF MY BEST SYCOPHANTS
ARE GENERAL MANAGERS

Wirtz's ownership has also been characterized by a devotion and accep-
tance of managerial mediocrity. This is seen most clearly in his incompre-
hensible devotion to Bob "Asleep At The Wheel" Pulford, who has been the
Blackhawks' GM and later executive vice president from 1977 through 2000
(and, ouch, still counting). Wirtz has stuck with Pulford through parts of four
decades now, long after it was clear that Pulford did not have what it took to
compete among the NHL's managerial elite. There have been few accom-
plishments in the Pulford era and the best of them were not even his doing.

---

[38]Tim Sassone, "Wirtz Ready to Spend? Seeing Will Be Believing," *Chicago Daily
Herald,* November 18, 1997, Sports, p. 8. Elsewhere, Sassone has written: "The 67-year-
old Wirtz has been his usual silent self during the first month of the Hawks' sad season."
Tim Sassone, "At Wit's End, Hawks' GM Has Run Out of Patience," *Chicago Daily
Herald,* October 30, 1997, Sports, p. 1. After calling the Blackhawks an NHL "laughing-
stock," Sassone wanted to know: "Isn't it time for Bill Wirtz to be heard from amid the rub-
ble of a season gone so terribly bad? Aren't those fans who are asked to fork over ungod-
ly sums of money for tickets to help pay Zhamnov's $3 million salary due some sort of
explanation or apology from the top for what's happened the last two seasons? You would
think so. Then again, these are the Blackhawks — smug, arrogant and without a Stanley
Cup since 1961." Tim Sassone, "Hawks' Problems Only Getting Worse with Each Passing
Day," *Chicago Daily Herald*, February 21, 1999, Sports, p. 3.

The best deal of the Pulford era was by Mike Keenan, who was general manager for a couple of seasons in the early '90s. Keenan dealt Denis Savard to Montreal for Chris Chelios in June 1990 — and two years later the Hawks played in their first and only Stanley Cup final since Pulford came to town 24 years ago.

And yet, incredibly enough, Pulford trumpets his achievements with the Hawks, proclaiming that the job he did was "great." In Pulford's mind, he has been an outstanding general manager, telling the *Daily Herald*, "I did a great job operating within the rules. We never missed the playoffs, we were competitive and we had some great teams."[39] Similarly, Pulford boasted to the *Chicago Sun-Times*: "I read an article recently about no one realizing the Boston Red Sox have had a lot of winning seasons because they haven't won a championship in longer than we haven't. But they were always competitive, like our teams were, and I'm here to get us back to that."[40] Pulford is right — the Blackhawks did appear in 28 consecutive playoffs from 1969 thru 1997. But since when is making the playoffs a mark of success? Patting himself on the back for this accomplishment is elevating mediocrity to a status it doesn't deserve. (Funny, Pulford never mentions the 28 years of playoff flops or the twenty-something consecutive years of ticket-price increases.) Pulford's very own words are damning to his own purported achievements: "The peers I grew up with, the (Harry) Sindens, (Bill) Torreys, (Cliff) Fletchers and (Glen) Sathers, etc., I think I have a great deal of respect from them."[41] In fact, Pulford's performance as GM pales in comparison these men's, each one of whom, except Sinden, has won the Cup at least twice.

But perhaps the biggest indictment of Pulford's tenure as Hawks GM and executive vice-president has been the immediate and drastic changes undertaken by new Hawks' GM Mike Smith soon after he was hired in November of 1999. At his first opportunity, Smith opted to overhaul entirely the Hawks scouting department and developmental system, hiring a new pro scouting staff. Under the watch of Pulford and Bob Murray (Pulford's disastrous handpicked successor as GM), the Hawks drafting incompetence was legendary. Over a period of twenty years from 1980 thru 1999, the Hawks had just two solid first-round successes — Denis Savard in 1980 and Jeremy Roenick in 1988 (and the Roenick selection was an accident).[42] In completely revamping

[39]Tim Sassone, "Pulford Still Feeling the Sting; Former GM Believes He's Not to Blame for Blackhawks' Woes," *Chicago Daily Herald,* November 13, 1997, Sports, p.1.

[40]Mike Kiley, "Who is the Real Bob Pulford," *Chicago Sun-Times*, Dec. 9, 1999, p. 152.

[41]*Id.*

[42]In Roenick's case, the Hawks blundered into success. Roenick was selected eighth overall, but the Hawks did everything they could to make Roenick's selection not happen.

the drafting operations, Smith pulled no punches about the pathetic state of affairs in the organization. "What we're doing here is we're building an organization," Smith explained, leaving unstated the bitter but obvious truth that the reason he has to build an organization is that none previously existed.[43]

The perfect Wirtzean sidekick, Pulford has always shared Wirtz's greed-twisted *Weltanschauung*.[44] It's not that either man is against winning *per se*, but on-ice excellence has always played second-fiddle to making the accountants happy. As Pulford acknowledged: "I tried to run it as if the club was mine. I ran this franchise as a business...and watched the bottom line."[45] Elsewhere, Pulford has said: "Some guy in Vancouver once wrote about me that I was a horse(bleep) GM because all I did was make money. I had to laugh because that's a back-handed compliment."[46] In December of 1999, Pulford really gave the game away when at a news conference announcing the firing of former GM Bob Murray, he spoke of the Hawks' rebuilding process and the goals he sought to achieve. "The job will be finished," Pulford declared, "when the stands are full." Sadly, win or lose, as long as the team brings in the paying customers, Pulford is satisfied. At the same news conference, Pulford said: "I feel good about the teams we put on the ice when I was in charge. I think we did a good job. Most of that period, the Stadium was full."[47]

Over the years, Wirtz has repeatedly portrayed his commitment to Pulford as "loyalty," but Wirtz's devotion is probably best explained as inertia that grows out of a paranoia and fear. GM Mike Smith is only the fourth so-called outsider in the last 45 years to be hired to run the Hawks. He follows in the footsteps of only Tommy Ivan (1954), Pulford (1977) and Mike Keenan (1990). It is not easy for a behind-closed-doors operation like Wirtz's to open its doors to new faces. It comes at a price. Independent minds create new ideas, make demands, threaten the *status quo*, create difficulties. Men

---

The Blackhawks much preferred the L.A. Kings' seventh-pick, Martin Gelinas, and unsuccessfully tried to trade up to select him. "We tried to trade up to get Gelinas and would have loved to have him," Wirtz said. Mike Kiley, "Blackhawks Trying To Arrange Ceremony To Retire Jerseys Of Hall, Esposito." *Chicago Tribune*, August 28, 1988, p. 6N.

[43]Tim Sassone, "Civics Lesson Hawks Plead Their Case To Restless Fans In Town Hall Meeting," *Chicago Daily Herald*, July 27, 2000, Sports, p. 3

[44]I admit it — I have no know idea what this word actually means. It's German for god-sakes!

[45]Mike Kiley, "Who is the real Bob Pulford?" *Chicago Sun-Times*, December 9, 1999, p. 152.

[46]Tim Sassone, "Pulford Still Feeling the Sting" *Chicago Daily Herald*, November 13, 1997, Sports, p. 1.

[47]December 2, 1999 Chicago Blackhawks' press conference announcing the firing of Bob Murray and the demotion of Lorne Mollekin to associate coach.

like Wirtz are extremely reluctant to put people into positions of power who could know too much and be troublesome. The result is stasis and a lack of fresh ideas. Management becomes a fortress, a tight-knit phalanx of like-minded people who aren't challenged or influenced by outside forces, with the inevitable result being no give-and-take, an absence of organizational creativity, and ultimate long-term futility.

Wirtz's managerial philosophy has also been marked by a ruthless, persistent ability to play it low, mean and ugly. One famous example of Wirtz's calculating pettiness is the revenge he took on Bobby Hull after Hull signed with the Winnipeg Jets. Wirtz used his friendship with Alan Eagleson to keep Hull off the 1972 Canada Cup team. Eagleson was in charge of organizing the 1972 Canada Cup between Canada and the U.S.S.R. He was also in Wirtz's pocket. Hull was the premier hockey player in the world in 1972 and was named to the Canada Cup team before he signed with Winnipeg. But after Hull defected to the rival league, Wirtz forced Eagleson to drop Hull (and other NHL "traitors") from the team out of spite. The Canadian public vehemently complained, but the NHL owners held firm. In his defense, Eagleson said he had no choice but to drop Hull and the others from the team, claiming that Wirtz and the other NHL owners had threatened to drop insurance coverage on the players if the WHA stars were allowed to play. But the excuse was a lame one. If the insurance guarantee was the only problem, there was plenty of excess money from tournament revenues to pay for the necessary insurance coverage to cover the risk of serious injury to a player.[48]

The Blackhawks' organizational hostility towards Hull has been exacerbated by Bob Pulford, who has done all he could to hurt Hull through the years. It is well known that Pulford and Hull have despised each other since their playing days in the NHL. With Wirtz's approval, Pulford left Hull unprotected in the 1979 expansion draft when Hull could have returned to Chicago and allowed fans to worship him one last time. Pulford also is the guy who inexplicably passed on drafting Brett Hull in 1984 out of the University of Minnesota-Duluth. Hull went to Calgary with the 177th pick after the Hawks had taken Ed Olczyk (3rd overall), Trent Yawney (45th), Tom Erickson (66th), Timo Lehkonen (90th), Darin Sceviour (101st) and Chris Clifford (111th).

Pulford also refused to trade for Brett Hull when Calgary came calling in 1988. The Flames came to the Hawks looking for a veteran goalie and a big defenseman. Would the Hawks want Hull for Murray Bannerman and either Gary Nylund or Behn Wilson, the Flames wondered? No, thank you, said Pulford. Calgary eventually dealt Hull to St. Louis with forward Steve Bozek

<hr />

[48]See William Houston and David Shoalts, *Greed and Glory: The Fall of Hockey Czar Alan Eagleson*, Warwick Publishing Inc., Toronto, 1993, p. 78-79.

for goalie Rick Wamsley and defenseman Rob Ramage. And in 1997 when Brett Hull was a free agent, Wirtz, Pulford and Bob Murray all apparently decided that Hull wasn't worth the free-agent money. Is there any wonder then why Bobby Hull refused to attend the Blackhawks' 75th year anniversary celebration when the Hawks honored their all-time greatest players.[49] Hull's laughable excuse for not attending was that he was busy selling cattle at his ranch in Canada, but everyone knew the real reason was to snub Wirtz and Pulford.

Another famous example of Wirtz's vindictiveness is the whole Bobby Orr incident, where Wirtz again used his friendship with Alan Eagleson to seek personal revenge on the Boston Bruins. In 1976, Orr signed a six-year, $3 million contract ($1.5 million guaranteed) with the Blackhawks, leaving the Bruins after an 11-year career and two Stanley Cups. In signing the Bruins' legend, Wirtz wasn't acting out of the best interests of the Blackhawks; he was acting out of spite and a personal vendetta against the Bruins. The signing of Orr was Wirtz's way of getting back at the Bruins for one the worst trades in NHL history, when in 1967 the Hawks traded Phil Esposito, Ken Hodge, and Fred Stanfield for Pit Martin, Jack Norris, and Gil Marotte. Wirtz always felt that Bruins GM Mike Schmidt had taken advantage of Hawks GM Tommy Ivan. Wirtz told sportswriter Russ Conway that signing Orr was "the best revenge of all, and Boston would get nothing in return."[50] Wirtz wanted to screw the Bruins so badly that he violated NHL rules by signing Orr to a deal before Orr's contract with the Bruins had expired. The Bruins were so outraged by Wirtz's tampering that they demanded Wirtz take a lie-detector test to prove he didn't tamper, but Wirtz never took the test, and for good reason, since Orr subsequently confirmed that the tampering did in fact occur.[51]

---

[49]At the 75th anniversary celebration, the Blackhawks announced their 18-man all-star Blackhawks team and unveiled a new commemorative statue outside the United Center. The 18-man all-star team consisted of Tony Esposito, Glen Hall and Ed Belfour in goal. The defense consisted of Chris Chelios, Doug Wilson, Pierre Pilote, Pat Stapleton, Bill White and Keith Magnuson. Centers were Stan Mikita, Denis Savard and Jeremy Roenick. Left wingers were Bobby Hull, Dennis Hull and Al Secord. Right wingers were Steve Larmer, Tony Amonte and Harold "Mush" March. Billy Reay, Mike Keenan and Bob Pulford were voted to the team as coaches.

[50]Russ Conway, *Game Misconduct: Alan Eagleson and The Corruption of Hockey*, MacFarlane Walters & Ross, Toronto, 1997, p. 143. For the Hawks, Norris turned out to be a fringe player; Marotte, an average defenseman, with limited mobility; and Martin, an effective but undersized centerman. In contrast, Esposito became one of the greatest scorers in NHL history and the dominant center of his era; Hodge was an All-Star right winger; and Stanfield, a solid second-line centerman.

[51]*Id.* at 142.

But the story doesn't end there. In the process of sticking it to the Bruins, Wirtz, together with his buddy Eagleson, who was Bobby Orr's agent at the time, screwed Orr out of millions of dollars. Evidence reveals that Alan Eagleson, as Orr's agent, never told Orr that the Bruins offered him 18.5 percent ownership of the Bruins' franchise if Orr would have agreed to resign with them. In fact, Eagleson had publicly maintained that the Bruins had stopped negotiating with Orr on December 10, 1975, when he reinjured his knee. But a now-public letter written by the Bruins on January 29, 1976 to Eagleson confirms that the Bruins made an offer to Orr through Eagleson of 18.5 percent ownership of the team. Orr, however, was never told of this offer. As Orr has made clear: "I never knew. There's no way I was given the details of that kind of offer. I think anyone would remember if he was offered a piece of a National League club."[52]

While there's no direct evidence that Wirtz instructed Eagleson to hoodwink Orr in his negotiations with the Bruins, the evidence offered in Chapter Six of this book has revealed that over decades Eagleson and Wirtz worked hand in hand to screw the players at the NHL negotiating table. It is thus difficult to dismiss the possibility, even likelihood, that Eagleson intentionally hid the Bruins' offer to Orr as a favor to his buddy, Wirtz. Nevertheless, Eagleson has vigorously denied that he "delivered" Bobby Orr to the Blackhawks as a favor to Wirtz. His denials, however, are nonetheless still incriminating to Wirtz. Eagleson has claimed that it was Wirtz who was doing him a favor in signing Orr. "The fact is," he said, "I went to Bill Wirtz and told him he owed me, and since Boston was throwing Bobby to the wolves with no guarantee, Bill Wirtz should do the right thing. Wirtz stepped up to the plate and paid $500,000 a year for a player we all knew wouldn't be able to play at any level of tough hockey."[53] According to Eagleson then, Wirtz didn't sign Orr out of vengeance but out of some undefined obligation to Eagleson himself — *"he owed me."* In the end, however, it is irrelevant whether Wirtz signed Orr out of a vendetta or a obligation to Eagleson. In either case, it appears that Wirtz's concerns were markedly distinct from the best interests of the hockey team itself.

A final example of Wirtz's thuggish manner can be seen in the firing of former Hawks coach Billy Reay. In 1977, after nearly 15 years and 1012 games as coach, the most by any Blackhawks' skipper in history, Reay returned to his apartment one Christmas Eve to find a note under his door informing him of his dismissal. Reay forgave Wirtz and stayed on with the

---

[52]*Id*. at 148
[53]*Greed and Glory* at 65.

Blackhawks' organization for several more years. The story has been called apocryphal by some defenders of Wirtz, but the late Bill Reay never denied it. In 1992, he told the *Chicago Tribune*, "Some things happen and in the long run it's probably for the best. Sure, it was disappointing, but it made no difference as to my feelings for Bill Wirtz."[54]

LET THEM EAT CRAPPY HOCKEY

Since he's not a public official, it's hard to accuse Bill Wirtz of shirking his civic duties, but in a sense his team is a public institution. The public square includes many parts of a community's civic life, and one important part is its professional sports teams. A sports team is not like every other business. Owning a team means, at least in part, being a caretaker of a public trust. Sports fans are dependent on owners in a way they are not on other businesses. Hopes rise and fall with an owners' commitments.[55] People put their trust and faith in a sports team owner to pursue excellence. As a result, an owner's personal economic interests should not trump all else. But for Wirtz they clearly do, and it's something he brags about, proudly asserting: "I'm a professional businessman. I run the Blackhawks as a business."[56]

In fairness to Wirtz, we all have a multiplicity of obligations and competing allegiances — to one's self, one's family, one's community. No one believes it's easy to balance these interests, and no one balances them properly all the time. But Wirtz's shame for decades now is that there has been no apparent effort to even attempt to balance these interests. The fans' interests and the community's concerns are off the map for him. And he basically admits this. When asked what his priorities in life were, Wirtz told the *Chicago Sun Times*, "family is first, business is second and nothing else is

---

[54]Robert Markus, "Wirtz Not Fan Favorite — But His Team Sure Is," *Chicago Tribune*, June 1, 1992, p. 1C.

[55]Robert Kraft, the long-time owner of the New England Patriots, said this about being a sports team owner: "I was on *This Week With David Brinkley* the morning of the Super Bowl, and I think it was Sam Donaldson who compared owning a sports team to owning a dry-cleaning franchise. But I told him it wasn't. I told him something I believe, that owning a team like the Patriots, any team, is being a caretaker of a public trust. And I take that very seriously. I walk through our parking lots before games sometimes, and I feel a tremendous sense of responsibility and accountability with these fans. This team matters to them, and mattered long before I came along. These Sunday afternoons are an important part of their life. We can't take those Sundays and just move on to the next city and not worry about the people we leave behind." Mike Lupica, *Mad As Hell: How Sports Got Away From the Fans And How We Get It Back*, G.P. Putnam's Sons, New York, 1996, p. 30.

[56]Robert Markus, "Wirtz Not Fan Favorite — But His Team Sure Is," *Chicago Tribune*, June 1, 1992, p. 1C.

third."[57] Nothing? After years of going without a Stanley Cup and now in the twilight of his life, one would think Wirtz would finally commit himself to winning the championship, but, in fact, as his own words attest to, Wirtz does not yearn for a Stanley Cup with any great passion. On another occasion, Wirtz confided to the *Sun Times* that there is very little in life he has a burning desire to accomplish, short of assisting his children with their businesses.[58] Sadly, in his actions and his words, Wirtz seems to cleave to the injunction of J. P. Morgan, who spoke for tycoonery everywhere, when nearly 100 years ago he said, "I owe the public nothing."

---

[57]Brian Hanley, "Hawks' Own Family Affair…Another Wirtz Plays Key Role for Hawks, Both On and Off Ice," *Chicago Sun-Times*, March 16, 1997, p. 18.

[58]Fran Spielman, "The Puck Stops Here; Bill Wirtz Gives Family New Legacy With Stadium," *Chicago Sun-Times*, August 28, 1994. People Plus, p. 1.

"Here I spend my whole life being an
unprincipled asshole and for what?
EVERYTHING! Ha! Ha!"

Chapter 8

Wirtz's Own
Personal Struggle

"I'll fight you both together if you want! I'll fight you with one paw tied behind my back! I'll fight you standin' on one foot! I'll fight you wit' my eyes closed!"

— *The Cowardly Lion*

It is almost impossible to read about Wirtz's profiteering, bribery, stealing, collusion, and skullduggery without asking, why? What explains his relentless pursuit of the almighty dollar? Why, when even the slightest restraint on his part, a magnanimous gesture or two, would have won him friends and gained him public favor, does Wirtz continue to exhibit an unquenchable lust for and ruthless pursuit of profits? Even given our society's own enormous appetite for material wealth, Wirtz's appetites seem extreme. From any rational perspective, he doesn't need to engage in the illicit activities and excesses detailed in this book. With every opportunity afforded to him, Wirtz would have been among our society's richest men without breaking any laws. With the understanding that the human heart is infinitely mysterious, I believe Wirtz's relentless pursuit of profits and corruption does make psychological sense when viewed as an effort to prove himself worthy of inheriting his family's fortune.

The children of the privileged elite often need to prove themselves, if not to others, then to themselves. It is not easy to inherit a family fortune, and it is often the case with the scions of second-generation billionaires that they feel compelled to prove they are worthy of the throne and tough enough to carry their father's mantle. In America, men prove their manhood by winning in the marketplace. No one wants to be seen as privileged and pampered, especially in a culture that mythologizes the self-made man. The offspring of vast fortunes are inescapably subject to the charge of getting to where they are because of nepotism. As a result, the sons of the wealthy elite are often driven to prove they are worthy of their very short climb to the top.

On top of this, Bill Wirtz's model for "manhood" was his father, Arthur, a fearsome, 6-foot-5, 340-pound man, who was famous for ruthless business dealings. Arthur Wirtz made his fortune in the midst of the Depression, preying on people's financial hardships to buy up properties at pennies on the dollar. Arthur was the quintessential dog-eat-dog, iron-fisted, unyielding businessman. Bill's own unrelenting pursuit of profits — both his pattern of corrupt activities and his practice of squeezing every penny he can from the Blackhawks — can be seen as an effort to prove his own comparable toughness.

We know little about Wirtz's upbringing, but we do know that as a boy and through early adulthood, Wirtz was an amateur boxer, a remarkably strange hobby for the son of a multi-millionaire. Not too many millionaire kids enter the ring for the fun of it. Its attraction for Wirtz would seem to be a place to prove his toughness. To this day, Wirtz still brags about the bloody barroom brawl that he got into with Rocky Marciano.[59] And even at 70 years old, Wirtz is still offering to knock people's lights out (mine especially). In a pre-season game between the Blackhawks and the Washington Capitals in September of 1999, Capitals GM George McPhee and Hawks coach Lorne Molleken exchanged blows in a post-game confrontation. In response, Wirtz offered up a challenge to the entire Washington Capitals management team to exchange dukes: "If these gentlemen want to come to Chicago and go in a room and turn the lights out, I'd be only happy to see them. I'll take our management against their management. Let's go in a room and have it out."[60]

Similarly, in the business world, Wirtz seems determined to show that his successes are the result of his own pluck and moxy, and not the result of inheritance or privilege. Fact is, no one has promoted the image of Bill Wirtz as a bottom-line, tough, aggressive businessman who is concerned first and foremost with money more than Bill Wirtz himself. I'm-a-professional-businessman-and-I-run-the-Blackhawks-as-a-business is as near a daily a mantra of Wirtz as we have.[61] Wirtz becomes virtually apoplectic when his business

[59]Fran Spielman, "The Puck Stops Here; Bill Wirtz Gives Family New Legacy With Stadium," *Chicago Sun-Times*, August 28, 1994. People Plus, p. 1.

[60]Tim Sassone, "Wirtz says he'd fire McPhee if he worked for Hawks," *Chicago Daily Herald*. September 28, 1999, Sports, p. 1.

[61]See Robert Markus, "Wirtz Not Fan Favorite — But His Team Sure Is," *Chicago Tribune*, June 1, 1992, p. 1C.

acumen is challenged. Once questioned about a particular business decision of his, he shot back angrily, "I know how to run a business. So I shouldn't be criticized by people who don't know how to run a business."[62] More than anything, these public declarations of his businesss skills seem to be pathetic reassurances to Wirtz himself of his own business acumen.

All indications are that as a young man Bill Wirtz was not terribly close to his father. Arthur Wirtz was a cold, workaholic man, who once even refused to speak to his son for three weeks after Bill purchased a house on credit, credit being something Arthur did not approve of.[63] Bill recalls that to speak with his dad during the week, he had to go to the Chicago Stadium: "My dad worked until 10 p.m. every night, so if we wanted to see him, we had to go to the Stadium."[64] The cold father even dismissed his son's professional desires. As Wirtz told *Chicago Magazine*, he graduated from Brown University in 1950 with a degree in economics and a minor in classics and desired to be an archeologist. "The economics was solely to assure my father that his tuition money wasn't being wasted," he says. "I was going to be a digger. My mother was thrilled. Dad gave me the silent treatment for about a month." Wirtz ended up joining the accounting firm of Peat, Marwick, Mitchell. But two years later, in 1952, Arthur asked his oldest son to join the family company and Bill turned him down, believing he was on his way up the partnership track at Peat, Marwick. "Dad looked at me like I was nuts," Wirtz recalls. A few weeks later, father sat down with his son again. "You're a damn fool," the father said. "And make no mistake. I'll never make this offer to you again." Bill relented. "What he was trying to tell me," he says, "was that I have a brother and sisters. That there was family equity to take care of and that I ought to do something other than think of myself. And I've never regretted a day."[65]

Wirtz's adoption of his public-be-damned business tactics similar to those of his father's can be seen as a way to stand side-by-side with his father and be the dutiful, good son. Here, it would seem that for Wirtz private virtue clashes head-on with public virtue: the good son honors the father by being like the father, but to be like the father he must violate certain of society's norms and endure the community's scorn. Thus, perversely, the harsh public

[62]Mike Kiley, "Angry Wirtz Blasts 'Cheap Shots' As Undeserved," *Chicago Tribune*, April 12, 1992, p. 7C.

[63]Jeff Bordon, "Banks, Booze, Buildings, Blackhawks Too: Inside The World Of Bill Wirtz," *Crain's Chicago Business*, April 14, 1997, p.1.

[64]Fran Spielman, "The Puck Stops Here; Bill Wirtz Gives Family New Legacy With Stadium," *Chicago Sun-Times*, August 28, 1994. People Plus, p. 1.

[65]Lisa Twyman Bessone, "Power Play," *Chicago Magazine*, January 1992 p. 122.

criticism and condemnation of Wirtz, which one might think would be a source of shame and a cause of discomfort and regret to him, is actually a badge of honor and serves a well-needed therapeutic function.[66] (The bill is in the mail.) It is a means to connect with his distant father, who was also the target of public condemnation. And by enduring the attacks and abuse, Wirtz can feel that he has earned his fortune, that a price has been paid for his success, and that his wealth has been legitimized.

As Wirtz enters the twilight of his life, most hockey observers are surprised that he has failed to commit himself to winning a Stanley Cup, especially given the Hawks' 40-year Stanley Cup drought. The *Chicago Daily Herald*'s Tim Sassone has asked:

> What's wrong with Wirtz anyway? Here's a man with a vast fortune of at least $600 million, who is approaching 70 years old and hasn't won a Stanley Cup on his watch as owner, and he's pinching pennies with a hockey club that has the most loyal fans in the city.[67]

But Wirtz's penny-pinching only appears confounding and inadequately motivated if one fails to understand how central to Wirtz's psychological make-up the need to prove his money-making prowess is. For Wirtz, there's no tragic, unresolved tension between a desire for profits and a desire for a Stanley Cup. Success on the ice would be nice, but it will not come at the expense of his profits, whose attainment serves a greater, more important objective, one rooted deeply in psychological necessity — to prove himself worthy of his inheritance.

Actually, it's hard not to feel a little sorry for the 70-something Wirtz. One can despise his bad decision-making and business ethics, but as the patriarch of one of America's richest families, he has been tormented by the need to prove himself his whole life. The wounds are readily apparent in his drinking and obesity. In our culture, the wealthy, successful businessman is often viewed as the mark of high achievement and independence — the very pic-

---

[66] Over the years, Wirtz actually seems to have embraced and fostered the public's scorn of him, as in his relishing of the nickname "Dollar Bill" (see fn. 12, p. 92 herein); his mockery of Blackhawks fans for their not booing him loudly enough (see Brian Hanley, "Hawks Look to Replace Shantz,"*Chicago Sun-Times*, March 21, 1998, p 94 Wirtz: "I used to be booed much louder at the old Stadium. I think our fans are getting weaker."); and his telling visiting teams that they shouldn't worry about playing the Blackhawks because "the loudest boos are always reserved for him." (see Lisa Twyman Bessone, "Power Play," *Chicago Magazine*, January 1992 p.123.)

[67] Tim Sassone, "Wirtz Blew It with Hull — So What Else Is New?" *Chicago Daily Herald*, July 5, 1998, Sports, p. 3.

ture of freedom — but Wirtz seems remarkably unfree. Unlike other businessmen who have made their money and feel competent and comfortable in
their achievements, Wirtz continually engages in unseemly, misguided acts of
overcompensation to prove his business acumen, acts that are totally unnec-
essary to maintain and expand his enormous wealth. In a sense, the fortune has
seemed to control Wirtz as much as, or more than, he has controlled the fortune.

"Your Honor, this mockery is a trial!"

Chapter 9

A Note On Satire

"Laughter is the best medicine...well, unless of course you've got bowel cancer and then nothing's gonna help."

— Norm MacDonald

The Blue Line was the unofficial Blackhawks' hockey program sold outside of all Blackhawks' home games from 1991 thru 1998. It competed against the Blackhawks' own official in-house program, called *Face-Off*. *The Blue Line* included the typical fare found in most hockey programs, including up-to-date rosters, statistics, and game-day information, but also featured satirical commentary about the Blackhawks and its management. At the risk of understatement, it could be said that the Blackhawks did not take kindly to the satire. They vigorously denounced *The Blue Line*, calling it "offensive," "profane," "crude," "sordid," "salacious," "obscene," "insulting," "malicious," "irresponsible," "unprofessional," "pornographic," vicious," and "defamatory." They claimed that the satire unfairly attacked Bill Wirtz's "character" and accused *The Blue Line* of "grossly misrepresent[ing]" everything Bill Wirtz stood for. They claimed *The Blue Line*'s objective was to "[tear] down a man." Bill Wirtz himself referred to *The Blue Line* as "a scandal sheet" and called the editors of *The Blue Line* "bungholer[s]." Under oath, the ever-classy Wirtz even stooped to questioning *The Blue Line* editors' heterosexuality, saying in his deposition, "I'm looking at you guys, and I don't think I want to bend down and get the soap." (Well, who even knew Wirtz used soap?) In addition, the Blackhawks argued that *The Blue Line* readers were being played for fools because *The Blue Line*, they claimed, did not provide readers with "constructive fan criticism" but instead "merely" "titillate[d] readers by maligning and lampooning Blackhawks representatives."[1]

The Blackhawks are absolutely right — the satire in *The Blue Line* was harsh and perhaps even vicious in its criticism of Wirtz. There is no getting around the aggressive, hostile intent behind it. In sharp contrast to the It's-Just-A-Joke School of Humor, satire comes under the category of the How-Sweet-It-Isn't School of Humor. Satire has a *j'accuse* element to it. It is meant to wound and embarrass its target. But just because words are harsh or hurtful doesn't mean they are ill-founded, ill-considered or unjust. Satire serves as a valuable means of social criticism, and even though it may be condemned by those who are its target, derisive laughter is a long-standing, respected, and perfectly legal outlet for less powerful individuals to express their scorn, disdain and disapproval towards those who abuse their power.

My response to the Blackhawks' denunciation of *The Blue Line*'s satire is: thank you very much. In denouncing the satire and tagging it with every pejorative adjective they could pay their lawyers to think of, the Blackhawks have paid us the highest compliment they could. If Bill Wirtz and the Blackhawks organization had enjoyed and embraced the critical satire in *The Blue Line*, something would be seriously wrong. The satirist's worst nightmare is that the intended victim of his satire fails to suffer emotional distress, but instead ignores the satirist or, worse yet, finds the whole thing merely funny and calls up the satirist, not to complain, but to ask for the original art work.

Perhaps the most succinct defense of the satirist's art comes from Herb Block, the dean of American political cartoonists. Block has been the editorial cartoonist of the *Washington Post* for over 50 years. (He was the first person to put the five o'clock shadow on cartoon images of Richard Nixon.) In explaining how he justifies making fun of people for a living, Block always tells the same story of the teacher who tried to instill in her students a love for animals. One boy told how he had taken in a kitten on a cold night and fed it. A girl told of how she had found an injured bird and nursed it back to health. When the teacher asked the next boy if he could give an example of his kindness to animals, the boy replied, "Yes, ma'am. One time I kicked a boy for kicking a dog."[2] In other words, there are many respectable ways to show one's love for mankind, and the satirist's art of denouncing corruption and the corrupt through ridicule is one legitimate way of doing so.

[1] See *Mark Weinberg and Blue Line Publishing v. Chicago Blackhawks Hockey Team, Inc.* case No. 96 L 1099, Circuit Court of Cook County, County Department, Law Division.
[2] Herb Block, *A Cartoonist's Life*, MacMillan Publishing Company, New York, pp.282-283 (1998).

The Blackhawks' denunciations of *The Blue Line*'s satire also reveal a flawed understanding of how commercial satire operates. The Blackhawks claim that the satirical attacks of Wirtz were out of bounds and unfair, but if the satire were regarded as such by the public at large, it would not have been so enthusiastically embraced. In the case of Bill Wirtz, the only reason he can be effectively lampooned is that he is so widely despised by Blackhawks' fans. If he weren't such an object of general contempt, he could not be ridiculed so easily. Many people think the satirist is a daring and risky social observer who refuses to worship at the pantheon of approved deities and has the temerity to cross those whom others are fearful to take on, but the dirty, little secret of commercial satire is that it is a wholly reactive art. The satirist is severely constrained in the targets he or she can effectively lampoon, and for all practical purposes must choose targets that society has already determined are deserving of critical commentary.

In order for any joke to succeed, there must be an absence of sympathy or even benign indifference for the target. No satirist, for example, can get away with harshly mocking objects of affection like the Pope, Mother Teresa, Christopher Reeves, Michael Jordan or others for whom there is even modest sympathy. The audience would rebel against such attacks — the ridicule would feel undeserved and offend the audience's sympathies and notions of fair play. Thus, in attacking *The Blue Line*, the Blackhawks are ignoring the person responsible for creating the market for the satire in the first place — Bill Wirtz. It is Wirtz's own deeds over 35 years that are responsible for the public's scorn for him. He alone is responsible for the public's disdain and disapproval. Though the satire found in *The Blue Line* may have helped concretize Wirtz's negative reputation, it is certainly not the cause of it.

The Blackhawks have also labeled the satire "obscene," by which they mean to object to *The Blue Line*'s use of certain four-letter words and sexually suggestive images and double entendres. Their hypocrisy, it must be said, is *fucking* astounding! Four-letter words and sexual references are apparently offensive to them, but the theft, bribery and predation on the part of their boss is perfectly acceptable? In condemning the use of four-letter words in the oh-so-filthy *Blue Line*, they reverse the order of serious crimes, picking apart *The Blue Line*'s satire for every naughty word but blinding themselves to the real indecencies at issue in the satire. The truth is, public morality and decency have nothing to do with the Blackhawks' objections to *The Blue Line*, and to hold themselves up as defenders of public morality is a sick joke. But then those in authority often cynically use the issue of "public morality" "decency" and "profanity" as an excuse to step on and crush those who cross them. In the former Soviet Union, the typical charge brought against dissident writers was that the writing was "pornographic," regardless of whether it was sexual or not. In his New York City obscenity trial in the 1950s, the comedian Lenny Bruce's satire was accused of being "obscene," but he knew the real objection was that he dared to mock the powers-that-be. Before sentencing, it was recommended that no mercy be granted Bruce because Lenny had shown a "lack of remorse." Lenny responded: "I'm not here for remorse, but for justice. The issue is not obscenity, but that I spit in the face of authority." The reality is, authority never likes to be criticized, mocked, or condemned, and will use any excuse it can to suppress criticism of it.

I know not everyone will find the *remarkably brilliant* satire that follows to be clever, witty, and urbane, but hopefully everyone can appreciate the serious purpose behind it. For ages, satire has been a way to condemn authority without violence or bloodshed. As Mark Twain recognized long ago, laughter is oftentimes the only "really effective weapon" against the rich and powerful: "Power, money, persuasion, supplication, persecution," can stir up hostility against humbugs. But laughter alone can blow them "to rags and atoms at a blast. Against the assault of laughter nothing can stand."[3]

---

[3]Peter Gay, *The Cultivation of Hatred: The Bourgeois Experience Victoria to Freud* Vol. III, W.W. Norton, New York, p. 373.

"Defamatory," "Obscene, "Crude," "Profane," "Vicious," "Pornographic" Satire from *The Blue Line*

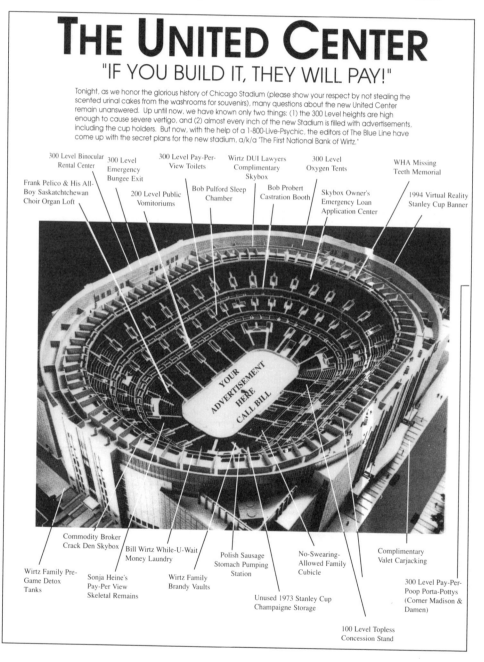

April 14, 1994

Blue Line Satire (cont.)

Form SLEE-Z 1040-DUI	Department of the Treasury—Internal Revenue Service Income Tax Return for Filthy Rich Paranoid Drunks With No Stanley Cups	1993	Department of the Treasury **Internal Revenue Service**

**Use the
IRS label**
(or a label
from your
favorite
bottle of
scotch)
	L
	A
	B
	E
	L
	
	H
	E
	R
	E
		Print your name (first, initial, last)
		    William W. Wirtz
		Home address (number and street.)
		    Madhouse On Madison
		City, state, and ZIP code
		    Chicago, IL. 60610
		Location of all secret foreign bank accounts
		    Geneva, Switzerland
		See **instructions** on back and in Form SLEE-Z booklet.
			Your social security number
			_ _ _ – _ _ – _ _ _ _
			
			Your spouse's social security number
			_ _ _ – _ _ – _ _ _ _
			
			**Your bartender's social
			security number**
			_ _ _ – _ _ – _ _ _ _

Fire Marshal Bribery Fund	Note: *Checking "Yes" will allow you to cram in 1,000 more fans per game.* Do you want $3 to go to this fund? ▶ If a joint return, does your spouse want $3 to go to this fund? ▶	**Your bartender's spouse's social security number** _ _ _ – _ _ – _ _ _ _

Filing Status	1 ☐ Tipsy ☐ Drunk ☒ Stupor ☐ Unconscious		

**Report
of All
Income**

2 The rape/exploitation of season ticket holders............	2	$16,750,000
3 Illegal racketeering and loan sharking..........................	3	$11,000,000
4 Skybox windfall...	4	$8,500,000
5 Overpriced merchandise at Hawkquarters.....................	5	$7,000,000
6 Advertisement on boards (seats, floors, ceilings, cup holders, etc.)	6	$1,500,000
7 Illegal use of players' pension fund.............................	7	$1,250,000
8 Scalping Ice Capades tickets.......................................	8	$12,000
9 Add lines 2 thru 8. **This is your gross income.**	9	$45,262,000

**Report
of All Ex-
penses
& Deduc-
tions**

10 Scotch..	10	$19,850,000
11 Players' salaries...	11	$17,700,000
12 Building inspector payoffs...	12	$12,500,000
13 Free pucks to Somalia..	13	$3,310,500
14 Yacht repair and wetbar expansion............................	14	$2,875,000
15 Hookers! Hookers! Hookers!....................................	15	$1,175,000
16 Pully's alarm clocks, nicotine patches, and milk money....	16	$750
17 Zamboni hubcaps..	17	$500
18 Charitable contributions to Maryville Academy............	18	$10
19 Add lines 10 thru 18. **This is your allowable deductions.**	19	$57,411,260

Figure Your Tax	20 **Tax.** Subtract line 19 from line 9 above and enter difference; (otherwise, enter result of most recent breathalizer test.)	-$12,149,260

Refund or Amount You Owe	21 If line 20 is a negative number, you're a bigger crook than anyone ever thought. Your trial date is set for next monday (which almost surely will *not* conflict with the Blackhawks playoff schedule.)

Sign your return (keep a copy of this form for your records.)	I have read this return. Under penalties of perjury, I declare that to the best of my knowledge and belief, the return is true, correct, and accurately lists all the amounts and sources of income I received during the tax year.

Your signature *William W. Wirtz*	Spouse's signature if joint return
Date 4/15/94	Your occupation Prick	Spouse's occupation Saint

Tax Preparer	This tax form was prepared by the law firm:	Gozdecki, Del Giudice, Fukem & Howe 221 N. LaSalle St., Suite 2200 Chicago, IL. 60601

For Privacy Act and Paperwork Reduction Act Notice, see page 4.	Cat. No. 12615V	Form 1040EZ (1993)

April 23, 1994

Blue Line Satire (cont.)

FAN'S OFFICIAL GUIDE TO BILL WIRTZ HAND SIGNALS

During the game, yachtsman Bill Wirtz uses an elaborate set of hand signals to communicate vital information to his handlers, toadies, lawyers and beer vendors located throughout the Stadium. To help you, the average fan, to better understand the complex "behind the scenes" machinations of running a professional hockey franchise, *The Blue Line* presents for the first time an official guide to deciphering these sophisticated hand gestures. **Warning**: these signals are presented for educational purposes only and are not intended for the home use of our audience. Unauthorized use of these hand signals may result in bouts of paranoiac self-delusion, inflated feelings of importance, irreversible liver damage, and a powerful craving to blow up old, historic landmarks. Proceed at your own risk.

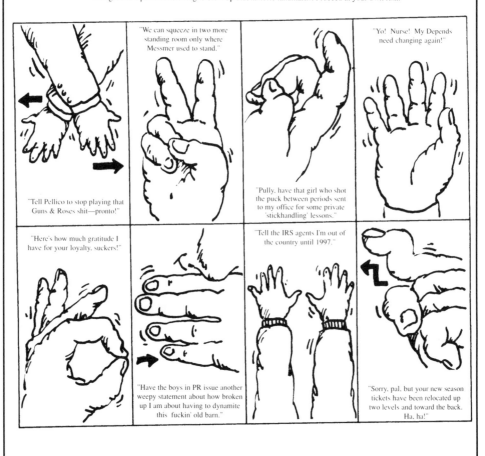

April 28, 1994

Blue Line Satire (cont.)

February 20, 1995

Blue Line Satire (cont.)

Blue Line Satire (cont.)

Blue Line **Satire (cont.)**

HOW TO SAVE MILLIONS IN REAL ESTATE TAXES!

$5,000,000 SAVINGS GUARANTEED!

Now Available On Tape — Bill Wirtz' Easy Three-Step Guide to Pulling Off An Incredible Real Estate Swindle

- **Step 1: Pay-Off Municipal and State Governement Officials to Insure Passage of Insane Tax Breaks;**
- **Step 2: Implement Forced Relocation (Ethnic Cleansing) of Surrounding Homeowners;**
- **Step 3: Continue to Make Huge Profits on Skyboxes and Concessions Without Significantly Increasing Your Reportable Net Income.**

TO ORDER CALL 1-800-*BUFU*

Darin Kimble on duty to take your call

Taxes? I don't pay no stinkin' taxes

AS NOT SEEN ON TV

Crazy Dollar Bill (pictured with loved ones)

Dear Sap:
In the aftermath of my recent health problems, I have decided to reveal <u>all</u> my real estate secrets to you, the average schmoe, for the low, low price of $19.95! I could very happily die without revealing any of my secrets for saving millions in real estate taxes, but this tape is my gift to the public for all the millions of dollars of tax burden I've shifted to them during the past year. Actually, I've thought about giving my secrets away for free, but I know people only value something when they pay for it.

WHAT'S MY SECRET?
This marvellous secret system of mine requires no tremendous intelligence (for I have none). It only requires a lust for money and the clout a $500 million inheritance provides. With this system, you'll be able to: a) limit your real estate taxes to a <u>fraction</u> of what other similar commercial properties are paying, b) receive "improper deductions" to artificially lower the overall fair market value of your property, and c) guarantee that these special legislative tax breaks continue for up to 24 years!

Here's some advance praise for this incredible tax saving system:

"One of the most incredible real estate tax giveaways ever!"
- Rep. Anthony Young (D)

""If I had known about this incredible system, I wouldn't need to float a fucking casino in my pond."
- Dick Duchusosois

"I'd like to stop this flagrant abuse of the system, but my hands are tied!" - Cook County Assesor

"Let's just sat we made Govenor Edgar an offer he couldn't refuse..."
- Jerry Reinsdorf

May 1, 1995

Blue Line Satire (cont.)

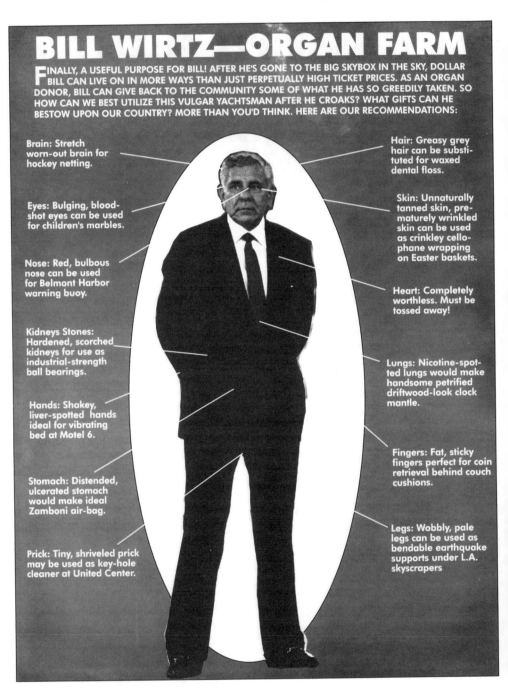

BILL WIRTZ—ORGAN FARM

FINALLY, A USEFUL PURPOSE FOR BILL! AFTER HE'S GONE TO THE BIG SKYBOX IN THE SKY, DOLLAR BILL CAN LIVE ON IN MORE WAYS THAN JUST PERPETUALLY HIGH TICKET PRICES. AS AN ORGAN DONOR, BILL CAN GIVE BACK TO THE COMMUNITY SOME OF WHAT HE HAS SO GREEDILY TAKEN. SO HOW CAN WE BEST UTILIZE THIS VULGAR YACHTSMAN AFTER HE CROAKS? WHAT GIFTS CAN HE BESTOW UPON OUR COUNTRY? MORE THAN YOU'D THINK. HERE ARE OUR RECOMMENDATIONS:

Brain: Stretch worn-out brain for hockey netting.

Eyes: Bulging, blood-shot eyes can be used for children's marbles.

Nose: Red, bulbous nose can be used for Belmont Harbor warning buoy.

Kidneys Stones: Hardened, scorched kidneys for use as industrial-strength ball bearings.

Hands: Shakey, liver-spotted hands ideal for vibrating bed at Motel 6.

Stomach: Distended, ulcerated stomach would make ideal Zamboni air-bag.

Prick: Tiny, shriveled prick may be used as key-hole cleaner at United Center.

Hair: Greasy grey hair can be substituted for waxed dental floss.

Skin: Unnaturally tanned skin, prematurely wrinkled skin can be used as crinkley cellophane wrapping on Easter baskets.

Heart: Completely worthless. Must be tossed away!

Lungs: Nicotine-spotted lungs would make handsome petrified driftwood-look clock mantle.

Fingers: Fat, sticky fingers perfect for coin retrieval behind couch cushions.

Legs: Wobbly, pale legs can be used as bendable earthquake supports under L.A. skyscrapers

May 21, 1995

Blue Line Satire (cont.)

BILLY'S GOT A BAD CASE OF...

PEANUTS ENVY

> What's the big fuss over a few lousy peanuts anyway? Hell, I haven't seen my nuts in over 20 years!

TOP 10 REASONS WHY I, KING BILL, HAVE BANNED PEANUT SALES FROM IN AND AROUND THE UNITED CENTER

10. Pully's getting too damn old to be picking up all those loose shells after every game.

9. Give fans affordable peanuts today, they'll expect free TV tomorrow!

8. Peanuts are for baseball–$8.50 Club Fajitas spell H-O-C-K-E-Y!

7. They taste terrible with scotch.

6. As my accountant has correctly pointed out, why buy expensive peanuts from a bum on the outside when you can spend a mere $6.00 for an Italian beef sandwich inside?

5. That traumatic childhood incident with serial fondler, Mr. Peanut.

4. If sidewalks become congested with peanut salespeople, where will all the crack dealers go? Who speaks for them? Huh?

3. Because sometimes you feel like a nut, sometimes you don't.

2. If those homeless peanut vendors make too much money, they might build their own stadium and buy their own hockey club and then where would I be?

1. *Because I can*, damn it!

"Sexiest Man of the Year"
— Fortune Magazine

October 15, 1995

Blue Line Satire (cont.)

─────── *Special Guest Editorial* ───────

"FREE T.V. WILL RUIN HOCKEY," SAYS ANONYMOUS FAN

Today, in America, something horrible is about to happen. Beginning this very afternoon — January 27, 1996 — FOX-TV will begin broadcasting NHL hockey games, including today's Blackhawks-Detroit Red Wings game, on free television. That's right, you heard me, I said FREE TELEVISION!

For twenty years now, critics have lambasted esteemed Blackhawks owner, William W. Wirtz, for his refusal to put Hawks games on free TV, but such criticisms are an unfair attack on a kindhearted, sweet, gentle, generous man who is wholly devoted to the well-being of his team, its fans, and the greater good of NHL hockey. While the arguments against putting hockey on free TV may not be popular or well known, they are extremely powerful. To begin, numerous government studies have proved that people who watch hockey on free TV tend to be: (1) stupid; (2) eat dirt; and (3) pee blood. And that's just from watching second-rate IHL hockey on third-rate local affiliates, like Channel 26 in Chicago, to pick just one example out of thin air.

If free hockey is available to every citizen, it's just a matter of time before the fragile social fabric that binds our society together starts to unravel. People sitting in their cold, isolated, radon-polluted basements, watching a flickering graven image, begin to lose touch with their fellow man. Communities begin to erode. Souls begin to wither. A gaping hole grows in the collective psyche. So sad, so very, very sad.

But there is still hope for us. For I have decided to lead a campaign to wipe out FOX-TV and its

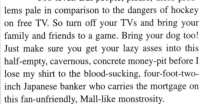

Anonymous Fan

ruthless, money-grubbing, Aussie carpetbagging owner, along with his satanic blue puck. But in order to do so, dear friends, I need your help.

First, turn off your damn TV sets. Second, show Rupert who's boss by coming down to the United Center and spending $75.00 on a ticket (not including parking, food, beer, souvenirs, etc.) to enjoy hockey the way the good Lord intended it to be enjoyed — in a luxury seat with your very own cupholder! And if you can't make it to the game because you are a pathetic cripple or too poor or whatever, then at least spend a few bucks to subscribe to cable TV. You'll feel like you've earned the right to watch hockey (away games only), not like a dirty, disgusting leach. I say, "Let them eat cable!"

There are a number of serious problems facing America today — violence, ignorance, drugs, poverty — all of which, by the way, can be found in the 300-level. But people, please, these problems pale in comparison to the dangers of hockey on free TV. So turn off your TVs and bring your family and friends to a game. Bring your dog too! Just make sure you get your lazy asses into this half-empty, cavernous, concrete money-pit before I lose my shirt to the blood-sucking, four-foot-two-inch Japanese banker who carries the mortgage on this fan-unfriendly, Mall-like monstrosity.

Turn off your goddamn TV's, you ungrateful bastards! I said turn them off. NOW!

The Blue Line is a fan's magazine and welcomes contributions from all points of view. No reproduction or reuse of this drivel is allowed except by the express written consent of the anonymous Blue Line publisher. E-mail your articles to blueline@mcs.com.

Blue Line Satire (cont.)

A BLUE LINE/CBS NEWS INVESTIGATIVE REPORT

SKYBOXES OF SHAME

Despite the belief that United Center skyboxes are populated by over-privileged fat-cats sucking down truckloads of hors d'oeuvres and chablis, the Blue Line Investigative Team® uncovered a very different reality...a reality that would make even Edward Murrow wince. Because right in our midst, in the supposed "paradise" of luxury skyboxes, there exists a shocking and scandalous truth, a truth that includes ritual abuse, willful neglect, rotting garbage and human waste. A truth we like to call the Skyboxes of Shame...

SKYBOX #302 - THE FORGOTTEN
This shocking photo was taken by an undercover *Blue Line* reporter posing as a leggy United Center cocktail waitress. Not only have these malnourished and illiterate lads been locked away in a dilapidated luxury skybox for years, but being located directly above Frank Pellico's organ loft, they've also had to endure the added insult of incredibly lame and listless organ music. According to our records, this skybox is owned by Sutter Farms. The DCFS is now investigating reports that these abandoned children are in fact the 76 missing Sutter brothers - the ones who *couldn't* skate! Oh, the shame!

SKYBOX #314 - THE EXPLOITED
The Andy Frains found a dozen men and women crammed together in sub-human living conditions in this $75,000-per-year Penthouse Skybox. It is believed to house the overflow undocumented housekeepers and groundskeepers of Blackhawk team owner "Dollar" Bill Wirtz. Subsisting on a forced diet of fried rats and intravenous drugs, these frightened illegals were barely able to muster the energy to speak, mumbling only in their pathetic broken English, "Bill Wirtz berry, berry good to us," and "peanuts berry, berry bad!"

SKYBOX #312 - THE PERSECUTED
Despite protests from such civil rights groups as Amnesty International, the United Center operates a minimum-luxury prison-camp skybox overflowing with peanut vendors, ticket scalpers, and Jeremy Roenick's agent. Many of these poor souls were unjustly sentenced after Chicago Blackhawk lawyers gained bogus convictions based on trumped-up war crimes charges. One prisoner told us that the skybox conditions are deplorable: the buffet is cold, the private toilet keeps running on after being flushed, and room service hasn't delivered bottled water in days. How can we allow this gross injustice to continue under our very noses? (Not pictured: Bruce McNall)

February 18, 1996

Blue Line **Satire (cont.)**

PULFORD MAKES BLOCK-BUSTER MEGA-DEAL!

Hawks GM Trades His Salami Sandwich for Peanut Butter and Jelly

In what may go down in Blackhawk history as the most stunning trade ever made, Chicago General Manager Bob Pulford pulled off a monster mega-deal yesterday that sent a salami sandwich and a Hostess HoHo to a 7-year-old grade schooler and brought a delicious-tasting peanut butter and jelly sandwich to the Hawks.

"I've been under a great deal of pressure to do something, anything," said an obviously relieved Pulford, "and I'm just happy that the trade went through and now I can go back to sleep. I'm pooped!"

Pulford had come under increasing criticism from fans and players alike for his inability or unwillingness to make the BIG TRADE. "Other teams, like St. Louis, have improved themselves dramatically for the playoff run," observed soon-to-be-ex-Hawk Jeremy Roenick, an outspoken critic of his team's clueless administration. "But now that we have the peanut butter and jelly sandwich on the roster, a proven performer with leadership qualities, we stand a much better chance at beating elite teams like Colorado and Detroit. It matches up well with Primeau's corned-beef sandwich." Although full details of the trade were not disclosed, playground sources say that Pulford made the food swap with first-grader Rebecca Feldman during Mrs.

DEAL OF THE CENTURY?

"She was the toughest negotiator I've ever encountered."
—Bob Pulford

"It was like taking candy from a baby."
—Rebeccah Feldman

Karnowski's spelling class. Feldman was reported to have had peanut butter and jelly every day this week and was more than happy to part with the sandwich.

Sources also confirm that Feldman's original offer included a bag of Doritos, but that she pulled the chips off the table in disgust after Pulford continued to waffle on the terms of the blockbuster deal.

Veteran playground observers believe that Feldman clearly got the better of the trade, not only obtaining a much more expensive sandwich dollar-for-dollar, but also netting a prized Hostess HoHo from the bumbling Pulford. Earlier in the day, a 3-way deal between Pulford, Feldman, and the LA Kings fell through when Pulford was unwilling to part with a Moon Pie straight-up for defenseman Marty McSorley.

With the NHL trade deadline fast approaching, Pulford was asked if any other hot deals were imminent: "All I can say is that I'm very close to pulling the trigger on a trade involving my wife's Chevy Vega to a band of wandering gypsies, but I can't say any more about it right now." The typically reticent Pulford did, however, go on to boast that the salami-for-peanut-butter trade speaks volumes about the Blackhawk organization's commitment to winning a championship this season.

The last laugh may be on Pulford, though, as the United Center peanuts ban technically extends to peanut butter, which means the new sandwich may not even be allowed into the Wirtz skybox, where Pully had planned to eat his new acquisition after a nap.

Special to **The Blue Line** *by Jay Manacotti (Slum Times)*

March 8, 1996

Blue Line Satire (cont.)

PRICELESS STAINED GLASS WINDOWS INSTALLED AT UNITED CENTER RINK

Wirtz replaces plexi-glass with church art in last-ditch attempt to avoid Hell

An antique collection of stained glass windows has been purchased by Blackhawks owner Bill Wirtz and installed along the boards of the United Center hockey rink, sources say.

The series of windows - which originally belonged to St. Peter's Basilica in Vatican City, Rome - are considered to be one of the eight wonders of the world, and were purchased by Wirtz for an estimated $1,774,000,000.00 and future considerations.

"I'll pay any price to get my poisoned soul into Heaven," said a nervous, chain-smoking Bill Wirtz. "And if I should end up in Hell, you'd better damn well believe I'll sue the Pope's ass to get my money back!"

The stained glass compositions not only depict Biblical scenes, but they also represent a spectrum of symbolic hockey meanings through various colors, says toupee-topped Blackhawk PR Director, Jim DeMaria: "White is the color of purity and also the color of 99.9% of hockey players and fans; gold signifies heavenly glory and our huge bottom line profits; red stands for the blood of redemption and for the blood on Enrico Ciccone's knuckles."

Some observers, however, are aghast that such beautiful and priceless religious pieces are being used for something as violent and profane as hockey. "Quite frankly, I'm appalled," said Cardinal Joseph Bernadin,

Super-fragile stained glass windows now grace the boards along the United Center ice rink in a pathetic attempt to curry favor with God.

speaking from the Chicago Archdiocese luxury skybox above the 300 Level. "These works represent the highest artistic expression of man's relationship with God, and now they're being used for something utterly vile and self-serving. Well, I got news for you, Wirtzy - you're still going to *Hell,* baby*!* Ha! Ha!"

Reaction from players has been mixed. Many have voiced their reluctance to drive an opposing player's skull through the new glass, especially when the Virgin Mary is staring you in the face. "It's spooky," said a visibly shaken Joe Murphy. "I would avoid going into the corners before, but I certainly won't go now with that icy virgin chick lookin' at me. Hey, she could use a little *headmanning,* if you know what I mean."

100-Level ticket holders also expressed concern over the new installation. Lisa Sorce, an Elmwood Park resident, said that while the stained glass provides the proper religious atmosphere to focus on quiet prayer, you can't "see for shit" when it comes to watching the on-ice action.

Despite these complaints, Wirtz says he has no intention of removing the new glass anytime soon: "It stays until I get into heaven or we win the Stanley Cup - whichever comes first, you ungrateful bastards." So consider it a permanent fixture, fans.

The above piece, entitled *The Baptisim of Jesus* (440 AD), was estimated to be worth $12 million before it was shattered into a million pieces by a Chris Chelios slap shot.

April 7, 1996

Blue Line Satire (cont.)

AN OPEN LETTER
TO SEASON-TICKET HOLDERS
From Blackhawks Owner
William W. Wirtz

Dear Season-Ticket Holder: October 11, 1996

It has come to my attention that some of you feel betrayed by my actions this past summer. I've heard that the combination of ticket price increases and the trade of Jeremy Roenick — and now the protracted negotiations with Alexei Zhamnov — has left a bitter taste in the mouths of many loyal Hawks fans.

Well, let me assure you that the Blackhawks are doing everything in their power to keep costs down and quality players on the ice. And let me say that, in spite of your incessant bitchin' and moaning, we've managed to disregard your concerns and get off to a good fiscal start anyway.

Maybe naive fuckheads like yourselves need to be taught a few simple, hard lessons about corporate life. But why waste my breath on fat, ignorant losers like you. You dumb bastards are nothing more than crap-eating, brain-washed puppets caught up in the mind-control game of the liberal Jewish media and their gay/Hollywood/Heroin-addict collaborators.

But rest assured, dear fans, that I go to sleep each night with a big, self-satisfied grin on my unnaturally-tanned face, secure in the knowledge that pathetic swine like you will keep coming back to the United Center even if I were to put huge piles of shit on the ice and charge you $50 to use the god-damned toilets, which I plan to do next year. Face it, buttwipes — you're the biggest fools that ever lived and you unconsciously enjoy getting screwed over again and again and again.

So go fist-fuck your hermaphrodite, in-bred sisters, assholes. Your piddling complaints roll off my back like water off a duck. Cancel your tickets for all I care. Why, I've got more money than you've ever dreamed of having, you lousy, little scum fucks. I'm rich, damnit! Rich! Rich! Rich! Ha! Ha! And you can suck my Forbes 400 cock!

I hope this has cleared the air. Thank you and God bless.

Sincerely,

William W. Wirtz

CHICAGO BLACKHAWK HOCKEY TEAM, INC.
1901 West Madison Street, Chicago, IL 60612-2459 phone (312) 455-7000
Season Tickets: 680 North Lake Shore Drive, 19th Floor, Chicago, IL 60611-3084 phone (312) 943-7000 fax (312) 787-5553

Blue Line Satire (cont.)

Not to be upstaged by the historic million-dollar endorsement deal signed recently between Wayne Gretzky and the Campbell Soup Company, Bill Wirtz has decided to launch his own line of private-label gourmet soups. Wirtz announced that all profits generated by his new *WirtZoup Inc.* venture will be donated to his favorite local charity: Himself.

WIRTZ SOUPS: YOU'RE SOAKING IN IT!

October 13, 1996

Blue Line Satire (cont.)

THE BLUE LINE TIMES

Vol. 6, #19   All the Hockey News that Prints   October 27, 1996

HOCKEY'S LEAST-POPULAR CARD IS GOING TO AUCTION

Rare Pulford Hockey Card Goes Up For Grabs At Sotheby's!

by T. Vidal Sassone
Special to The Blue Line

Pully is finally on the trading block.

Unfortuantely, it's not the real-life (sic) Bob Pulford, but rather a rare, mint-condition Bob Pulford hockey card, circa 1956 , that is up for auction Monday at the New York branch of Sotheby's International Auction House. The very same card fetched nearly 2¢ in 1991, and is widely blamed for causing the overall crash in the sports memorabilia market. "It's the Edsel of the sports card field," groaned Brad Finklestein, president of the Single Men's Memorabilia Association.

Its recent history—seven kids have owned it since 1995—illustrates the volatility of the sports-collectibles industry and the broad unpopularity of the Pulford card. In particular, hockey cards (except those featuring Super Mario or a topless Manon Rheaume) have plummeted in price over the past five years. However, the pre-sale estimate by Sotheby's for the Pulford card—0¢ to 0.5¢—is optimistic and reflects recent speculation about Pulford's current state of health.

How did such a nice little hockey card come to be utterly valueless, not even worth the cheap cardboard it was printed on? First of all, we're talking Bob Pulford here. Pulford was one of the most colorless, boringly predictible players ever to lace up the skates. He played for the Toronto Maple Leafs, a team comprised of scar-faced, brain-dead canucks, and Pulford

TOPPS

THE BOB "I CAN'T BELIEVE IT'S NOT TOILET PAPER" PULFORD HOCKEY CARD

was consistently chosen Least Likely to Get Laid each year in a team vote.

But what really makes the card worthless is its smell. Legend has it that Pulford, worried that he would encourage young fans to smoke cigarettes, had his card pulled from hockey card cigarette packs throughout Canada. More likely was the fact that Pully was too cheap to buy toilet paper in those days, and used the cards for, well, you know what.

What will Pulford bring this time around? Predictions are clouded by this week's news that the card may be a fake. However, memorabilia insiders say that shouldn't affect the card's value one bit. "In fact," says one unnamed source, "if it were a forgery, it would probably increase the final sale price ten-fold."

One potential bidder, Billy Spriggs, age 8, of Moose Jaw, says that he's not concerned about the authenticity or popularity of the Pulford card, because he only plans to put it on the spoke of his bicycle for that 'rat-tat-tat' noise. And odds are that Billy may come up big: "I've left a bid for 3¢, which means they'll have to pay me to take it off their hands," says the savvy Spriggs. "I have a better than 50-50 chance of getting it for that."

Regardless of who ultimately gets stuck with the accursed card, Pulford says he'll be happy to see it go to a good home, adding, "Heck, if I were to croak tomorrow, I'd bet that damn card would double—maybe triple— in value overnight!"

Buddy, can you spare a nickle?

Blue Line Satire (cont.)

BISMARCK CONCESSIONS
proudly announces...

FOOD SERVICE WITH A HOLE NEW ATTITUDE!

H ey, Hawks fans. Tired of the same old stadium food served by the same old miserable, minimum-wage stadium drones?

Well, here at the United Center, a new level of personal "service" is about to become legal.

Thanks to a joint-venture with our friends at Hooters®, Bismarck Food Concessions is sportin' a whole new attitude!

Oh sure, Bismarck will still pop the damn corn, heat the rubbery pretzels, and serve up over-priced cups of your favorite, watered-down brew.

But in addition, you'll now get eye-poppin', zipper-risin' service that'll have you begging (we hope!) for sloppy seconds!

And all for a modest PSL (Personal Slut License) fee of only $50,000!

Our foxy food nymphs are ready and eagerly waiting for the crush of hot & hung-ry Hawks fans. Heck, for a minimal extra fee, they'll even bring refreshments right to your seat for a little "lap-noshing" action!

We hope this makes your night out at the game a little more enjoyable. We know it'll be a helluva lot more profitable!
—HAWKS MANAGEMENT

JUST SOME OF OUR NEW MENU ITEMS:
- CONNIE'S DEEP-THROAT PIZZA ($200/hr.)
- STRAP-ON POLISH ($300; $400 IN THE BUN)
- SWOLLEN JUGG O' MILK (WITH SOUVENIR D-CUP)
- SPLIT OCTOPUS AU JUS ($Market$)
- CLUB VAGITAS ($45/Piece)
- SURGICALLY-ENHANCED MOUNDS BAR (2 for $25.00)
- MAI TAI ME UPS ($12.50)
- JAMAICAN WHO JERKS YOUR CHICKEN ($50/hand)

(pictured) **Candi Sweet, Fry-Vat Pet-of-the-Month**

November 7, 1996

Blue Line Satire (cont.)

Blue Line Satire (cont.)

Blue Line Satire (cont.)

A *BLUE LINE* TRIBUTE:

BEHIND THE SCENES

In life, we often fail to recognize the many important contributions made by the "little people," those faceless masses who toil fruitlessly in thankless, dead-end jobs. To remedy this injustice, the *Blue Line* is pleased to present this special tribute to the forgotten men and woman of the Chicago Blackhawks. It is due largely to their tireless, behind-the-scenes efforts that a Hawks game is an experience that will last a lifetime, even after many years of painful electro-shock therapy. Our hats off to you--the real Hawk Heroes!

William Overdew
PLAYOFF TICKET
PRICE HIKER

Raymond Bees
JIM DEMARIA'S HUMAN
TOUPEE RACK

Zeppo Sutter IV
TV BLACKOUT TECHNICIAN

Wayne Bleedingstool
WIRTZ PERSONAL BARTENDER/
SENIOR CONSULTANT

Daag Butterdick
CANADIAN HOOKER
ADVANCE SCOUT

Herb Evore
WIRTZ BACK-UP BARTENDER

Sam Pellcase
WIRTZ BARTENDER TRAINEE

Dietrich Speer
CHIEF POLITICAL BRIBE
COURIER

Antonio Flare
BOB PULFORD SPINE LOCATER

Emile Tickets
WIRTZ YES MAN

Richard Wiper
300-LEVEL URINAL CAKE
REMOVAL ASSISTANT

"Nick"
LUXURY SKYBOX
COCAINE MULE

OTHER KEY BLACKHAWK ORGANIZATION PERSONNEL (Not Pictured): Vladislav Tretiak (Wirtz Family Vodka Advisor), Aaron Tyres (Zamboni trainer), Jack Hoffa (Shoot-the-Puck babe bodyguard), Buster Chops (Ethan Moreau Tooth Spotter), Boris Yeltsin (Wirtz designated liver donor), J.D. Salinger (Public Relations), Orenthal J. Simpson (Peanut Vendor Exterminator), Susan Age (Beer Diluter), Dee Jenerett (24-hour on-call Wirtz bail bondsman), Allen Rench (JumboTron Plumber), Steven Hawking (Brent Sutter speed skating coach), Polly Esterpants (Russian player's fashion consultant), Ray Charles (Goal Judge supervisor), Cam Russell (Visitor's lockerroom jockstrap valet), Barbie Kewh, Esq. (Bismarck Foods product liability defense lawyer), Don Cherry (Team psychiatrist), Betty Wedder (Bob Probert drug test substitute urinator), Darryl Sutter (Cow milking coach), Dale Tallon (Team Caddy), Dr. Kevorkian (Special Liaison to Ron Salcer), Steven Kohn (Team Proctologist/Wirtz Real Estate Broker), Brooke Faceshields (Tony Amonte split-ends coach), Mike Keenan (Scapegoat Emeritus), Bubbles the Chimp (Enrico Ciccone stunt double), Jimmy Swaggert (Team Chaplin), Dr. Ruth (Fight Doctor), Jenny McCarthy (Puck Heater)

Blue Line Satire (cont.)

April 9, 1997

Blue Line Satire (cont.)

WIRTZ CO.: THE QUIZ

EDITOR'S NOTE: You can just imagine the waves shock and disbelief that swept through *The Blue Line* offices this past Monday as we read (with mounting horror) the *Crain's* cover story about Bill Wirtz and the Wirtz Corp. empire (see opposite page). Who knew? All along we believed Bill Wirtz to be what he presented to the public: a poor but honest businessman, trying to make payroll each week and stay off welfare, pouring every last cent from his tiny Subway sandwich franchise into his beloved hockey team. Bill Wirtz, fighting valiantly on behalf of Hawks fans to keep up with those better-heeled owners in Florida, Detroit, New Jersey, Colorado and Dallas. But now, sadly, thanks to the penetrating investigatory work of *Crain's Chicago Business*, our world has been turned upside down. Could Bill actually have *hundreds* of *millions* of dollars? Could he be operating the Blackhawks with the same iron-fisted, bottom-line philosophy as he does his myriad of banks, insurance companies, real estate holdings, horse farms and liquor distributorships? Disillusioned, we are only slowly coming to grips with our naivete, wondering how we could have been so terribly mistaken about this beautiful man. And what about you, dear reader? How much do you really know about this "Dollar Bill" character? To find out the answer, we urge you to take this Bill Wirtz quiz. Just do yourself (and the guy sitting in front of you) a favor--don't start eating those nachos until you've finished.

• •

1. Wirtz Corp. generated (conservatively) how much revenue in 1996:
1. $610.5 million;
2. $918.3 million;
3. (Oprah + Tiger Woods) x Bill Gates = Wirtz Corp.

2. 'Big Daddy' Arthur Wirtz lived by what motto:
1. "Buy smart and hold;"
2. "Cash and equity;"
3. "Sonja Henie was one hot little piece of ass!"

3. When eldest son Rockwell 'Rocky' Wirtz said that the Wirtzes "wear their fur on the inside," he meant that:
1. The Wirtzes don't parade their wealth in public like some rich people;
2. The family's 124-foot yacht is very modestly appointed;
3. They wear fur coats inside their luxury skybox, sweating dollars.

4. The 'W' in William W. Wirtz stands for:
1. Wadsworth;
2. Willmington;
3. Herff.

5. A graduate of Brown University, Bill Wirtz began his career as a:
1. CPA with Peat Marwick;
2. Clerk at the Chicago Board of Trade;
3. Multi-millionaire.

6. Throughout their vast banking empire, the accomplishment the Wirtz family is most proud of is:
1. The 12.5% return on equity at their First Security & Trust Bank in Elmwood Park;
2. The 2.8 million shares they own in Milwaukee-based Firstar banks;
3. Instituting a $3 service fee for cashing retirees' social security checks.

7. Arthur Wirtz launched the Wirtz financial juggernaut by buying up lakefront property in the 1930's. He accomplished this by:
1. Paying nickels on the dollar for distressed real estate;
2. Capitalizing on the broken dreams of the common folk crushed by the Great Depression;
3. Sitting on people.

8. Rival real estate firms characterize the 100+ apartment buildings owned by the Wirtz clan as 'cash cows' due mainly to:
1. The fact that they are debt-free and owned out right;
2. Wirtz's refusal to spend any money for upkeep on the crumbling structures;
3. Crack ho's.

9. Wirtz liquor distributors control 54% of the distilled spirits and wine business in Illinois. Most of this overpriced booze is consumed by:
1. Affluent yuppies in downtown restaurants and nightclubs;
2. Hapless fans at Bulls and Blackhawks games;
3. Bill.

10. Bill Wirtz refuses to allow the broadcast of Blackhawks home games because:
1. It would be an affront to season ticket holders;

2. It would be an affront to his parking lot and concession interests;
3. It would be an affront to knowledgeable hockey fans watching at home.

11. When Bill Wirtz says it's okay to occasionally suffer a 'gentlemen's loss,' he means:
1. It's all right to suffer a modest financial loss from time to time;
2. If you are highly diversified some investments will inevitably turn sour;
3. It's perfectly acceptable to double-cross the fans by trading away Jeremy Roenick.

12. Bill Wirtz's partner in the United Center, Jerry Reinsdorf, said Wirtz is "one of the smartest people I've ever known." This assessment is based on:
1. Wirtz's ability to cut to the heart of a matter;
2. Wirtz's skill at grasping complicated financial technicalities;
3. Wirtz's knack for sucking money out of fans' wallets.

13. The Wirtzes are often quick to cite that they give away millions to local charities. Which one is Bill's favorite:
1. Maryville Academy;
2. Ronald McDonald House;
3. The Hooters Foundation.

14. Bill Wirtz is said to be seething at Mayor Daley and Governor Edgar over their plans to:
1. Build a publicly-financed domed stadium to compete directly with the United Center;
2. Attempt a land grab of Wirtz-owned property on Chicago's west side;
3. Pass a new law lowering the legal blood alcohol limit to .08.

15. With Wirtz Corp. growing at a rate of 7% to 10% annually, by the year 2097, they will likely:
1. Have net assets in excess of $762 trillion.
2. Own every bank and apartment building still standing in the tri-state area.
3. Still claim to be a second-line center away from winning a fourth Stanley Cup.

16. When Ernest Gates, president of a west side community development group, said that "a handshake works for [Wirtz]," he was referring to:
1. Wirtz grudgingly delivering on promises for west side community investment;
2. Gaining a commitment from a reluctant Wirtz to donate funds for replacement housing for displaced residents;
3. How Wirtz cleans off after taking pee.

17. Bill Wirtz claims to have quit drinking and given up a 5-pack-a-day cigarette habit. What has he replaced these vices with:
1. Gardening;
2. Butterfly collecting;
3. Lying.

18. Bill Wirtz says his family has always taken hockey "very seriously." This is best demonstrated by:
1. Their commitment to developing youth and fairly compensating top talent;
2. Building a state-of-the-art hockey facility for players and fans alike;
3. Protecting season ticket holders from the growing peanut vendor threat.

Answers: #3 is the correct answer for all of the above questions. For proof, see the article entitled, "Up Tours, Chicago," by Jeff Borden in the April 14th issue of Crain's Chicago Business.

April 20, 1997

Blue Line Satire (cont.)

Blue Line Satire (cont.)

THE BLUE LINE TIMES

| Vol. 7, #1 | All the Hockey News that Prints | October 9, 1997 |

BILL WIRTZ TAKES UP TED TURNER'S CHALLENGE!

HAWKS OWNER TO DONATE OVER $1 BILLION TO FAVORITE CHARITIES

In a shocking development that occurred earlier this week, Chicago Blackhawks owner, Dollar Bill Wirtz announced he will accept billionaire Ted Turner's public challenge made last month to this country's super-rich to respond to the plight of the world's needy and forgotten millions. In making his challenge, Turner donated $1 billion to the United Nations to fund humanitarian efforts around the world and urged his fellow billionaires to follow suit. Dollar Bill said he will not be outdone by some "dumb baseball owner " and has decided to exceed Turner's $1 billion gift with a gift of $1 billion and 1 cent. Not surprisingly, however, there were a few very minor strings attached to the Wirtz donation. Wirtz stipulated that his money be spent only on specific "humanitarian" aid programs, ones that he personally approved of. *The Blue Line* has obtained a list of the charities approved by Mr. Wirtz and the amounts earmarked for each:

• $1,500,000 for birth control education pamphlets for Sutter family.
• $2,000,000 to restock Mother Teresa's food bank with leftover Connie's Pizza slices.
• $4,500,000 for new cellular pagers for unresponsive NHL officials who don't return calls to confirm god-damned blockbuster trades.
• $3,000,000 for gourmet food stamps for Peter Pocklington.
• $1,000,000 for medicinal crack for Bob Probert.
• $6,750,000 to halt global warming of national Schlitz supplies.
• $2,000 to help reduce e.coli outbreaks at Cheli's Chilli.
• $1,250,000 to provide Bismarck® sugar-water baby formula to third world nations.
• $4,000,000 for the Bill Wirtz Endangered Species Supper Club.
• $1,250,000 reward for Gary Bettman--dead or alive.

"I'm tanned, I'm rich, and I'm here to help pathetic losers like you!"

• $100,000 for the Stuck in the 50's Preservation Society.
• $6,000,000 for land mine development around Joe Louis Arena.
• $3,250,000 for Amnesty International's Alan Eagleson fund.
• $5,000,000 to airlift Andy Frain Peacekeepers into Bosnia.
• $50,000 to fund new humanitarian physician group, Proctologists Without Borders.
• $100 to feed starving Supermodels.
• $2,250,000 to build new irrigation canals in United Center bathrooms.
• $8,500,000 for research into pig liver transplants for aging rich alcoholics.
• $2,350,000 for the Hockey Head-Start Program (formerly known as the Bob Pulford Hire the Handicapped Program).
• $400,000 to test dangerous new AIDS vaccine on hockey agents.
• $5,000,000 to develop new peanut-eating pesticides.
• $7,000,000 to finance child-labor Zamboni factory in Amazon rain forest.
• $4,750,000 for heated speculums in Canadian abortion clinics.
• $65,000 for D.A.M.M. (Drunks Against Madd Mothers).
• $5,000 to develop state-of-the-art space program in Ethiopia.
• $2,500,000 to build luxury retirement prison for dear, dear friend, Pol Pot.
• $9,400,000 to wipe out deadly eblueline virus in Chicago.
• $5,500,000 start-up money for the Internet Smut Merchant's Association.
• $9,500,000 annual donation to Alcoholics Unanimous.
• $3,750,000 for the Gordie Howe W.A.D. Foundation (Wearer's of Adult Diapers).
• $75,000 to air-drop Fen-Phen to starving Kurds in Iraq.
• $500 for emergency penicillin shots for Joe Murphy.
• $2,500,000 to study effects of scotch farts on ozone layer.
• $47,000,000 for the 'Save The Bill Wirtz Swiss Bank Account' Superfund.

Blue Line Satire (cont.)

Blue Line Satire (cont.)

October 19, 1997

Blue Line Satire (cont.)

If you sweat when playing hockey, shouldn't your stickmaker sweat a little, too?

In this dehumanized age of automation, WIRTZWOOD™ still makes hockey sticks the old-fashioned way. By hand. Using underpaid workers. In appalling conditions. In underground Canadian sweatshops.

Phil (right) double checks each new WIRTZWOOD™ hockey stick for quaslity. And he'd better, because if just one stick gets shipped that doesn't meet with Bill Wirtz's exacting standards, he gets an ass-whipping like you've never seen.

87-year-old Pierre (left) gently sands each WIRTZWOOD™ hockey stick into perfect shape and balance. He's been doing this for more than 80 years, 16 hours a day, seven days a week. He's lucky to be making the 6¢ an hour Mr. Wirtz pays him, the lazy bastard.

"My GOAL is to exploit the weak and PASS the savings on to you!"
- Bill Wirtz, President, WIRTZWOOD™

WIRTZWOOD™

Made From 100% Stolen Construction Site Lumber

October 24, 1997

Blue Line Satire (cont.)

Appendix

Appendix A
Exchange of Letters between
Chicago Blackhawks and *Chicago Tribune*

The Blue Line has not been the only publication the Blackhawks have objected to over the years. In 1998, Peter Wirtz wrote a letter to the editor-in-chief of the *Chicago Tribune*, Mr. Howard A. Tyner, attacking *Tribune* columnist Steve Rosenbloom for what Peter called Rosenbloom's below-the-belt, demeaning attacks on his father. Since arriving in town in 1991, Rosenbloom, like all other sportswriters covering the Blackhawks, has been a harsh critic of Wirtz. Rosenbloom has noted that the very term "Blackhawks management" is an oxymoron. He has ridiculed Wirtz's capacities as owner, asserting that "If the NHL really wanted to crack down on obstruction, it would make President Wirtz sell the Blackhawks." He has mocked Wirtz's infamous greed, claiming that "Wirtz has UPC codes on all his singles to make sure no one takes them." And he has punctured Wirtz's repeated false displays of sympathy for Blackhawks' season-ticket holders, as when, in response to a late 1990's Blackhawks press conference, Rosenbloom quipped, "Quick, somebody roll out Bill Wirtz so he can mumble some more about how he's looking out for his precious 'season-reservation holders.'" In response to the Blackhawks' letter attacking Rosenbloom's satirical jibes at Wirtz, the *Tribune*'s Howard Tyner wrote a letter back that effectively told the Blackhawks — you reap what you sow.

Appendix A

Chicago Blackhawks and *Chicago Tribune* letters

April 21, 1998

Mr. Howard A. Tyner
Vice President and Editor in Chief
Chicago Tribune
435 North Michigan Avenue
Chicago, Illinois 60611

Howard,

For the Blackhawk Organization, this past season has been one of many disappointments. For the first time in 29 years, we have missed the playoffs. We deserve many of the critiques that have been directed towards our organization. However, the constant barrage of "below the belt" shots that Steve Rosenbloom has taken at us, is at times, unbearable. I do not understand the humor or satire he uses when directed towards the Blackhawks. He seems to have a vendetta against our organization. His reference to Bob Pulford and my father, William Wirtz, as "morons" (Sunday 4/19/98) really turned my stomach. My father is in both the NHL and USA Hockey Hall of Fames. He has dedicated his life to the great sport of hockey. He does not deserve to be called a "moron".

In the same article, Rosenbloom referenced Brent Sutter whom is retiring after this season, what is the purpose of taking a shot at a player who has given this sport his blood, sweat and tears over the past 17 years. Brent is a real credit to our sport and does not deserve these types of comments.

I have enclosed a sampling of past articles by Steve Rosenbloom, and I respectfully ask that you review them. Why does he need to constantly criticize our organization in this demeaning manner? It is one thing to criticize the team or a player for not playing up to a certain level, it is another to constantly stick a knife in and twist it.

Thank you for your consideration in this matter.

Best regards,

Peter R. Wirtz
Vice President of Marketing

Cc: Jack Fuller, President and Publisher
        John Cherwa, Sports Editor

CHICAGO BLACKHAWK HOCKEY TEAM, INC.

1901 West Madison Street, Chicago, IL 60612-2459 phone (312) 455-7000
Season Tickets: 680 North Lake Shore Drive, 19th Floor, Chicago, IL 60611-3084 phone (312) 943-7000 fax (312) 787-5553

Appendix A

Chicago Blackhawks and *Chicago Tribune* letters

Memo

To: William W. Wirtz
Bob Pulford
Bob Murray
Gene Gozdecki
Jim DeMaria

From: Peter R. Wirtz

Date: 05/06/98

Re: Response letter from Howard Tyner

Attached please find a copy of the response I received from Howard Tyner, Editor of the Chicago Tribune, regarding my April 21, 1998 letter (see attached). I am a bit perturbed by his short and uncompassionate response. As you will read, he mentions that "Steve is a passionate fan of ice hockey who clearly was disappointed by this year's performance by the Blackhawks." If Steve is so passionate, why did he not attend <u>one</u> of our games this past season?

In my opinion, Steve Rosenbloom is a "cheap-shot artist" who has been very destructive towards our organization and it is obvious that he has the support from the management at the Tribune.

CHICAGO BLACKHAWK HOCKEY TEAM, INC.

1901 West Madison Street, Chicago, IL 60612-2459 phone (312) 455-7000
Season Tickets: 680 North Lake Shore Drive, 19th Floor, Chicago, IL 60611-3084 phone (312) 943-7000 fax (312) 787-5553

Appendix A
Chicago Blackhawks and *Chicago Tribune* letters

435 NORTH MICHIGAN AVENUE
CHICAGO, ILLINOIS 60611-4041

HOWARD A. TYNER
EDITOR

TELEPHONE
(312) 222-4331

May 1, 1998

Mr. Peter R. Wirtz
Vice President of Marketing
Chicago Blackhawk Hockey Team, Inc.
1901 West Madison Street
Chicago, IL 60612-2459

Dear Mr. Wirtz:

Steve is a passionate fan of ice hockey who clearly was disappointed by this year's performance by the Blackhawks.

The recent management changes, I am sure, will bring about results that give Steve no room for criticism.

Best wishes,

cc: Jack Fuller
       John Cherwa

Appendix B
Copy of Letter Written by Bob Pulford to Ontario Court Attesting To Alan Eagleson's "Unquestionable" "Integrity."

ROBERT J. PULFORD
Senior Vice President

December 5, 1997

To Whom It May Concern:

I first met Eagleson as an opposing lacrosse player when I was 18 years old. As time passed we become good friends. Eagleson went on to law school to become a young lawyer in the same town I lived in. I became a professional hockey player in 1956. Between 1956 and 1967 Eagleson advised me during contract negotiations.

Eagleson and I would spend hours together discussing hockey. I represented my team on the player owner council in the NHL and would tell Al of how difficult it was to accomplish anything through this council.

The relationship between owners and players was not getting any better. The NHL pension was poor, benefits were non-existent and it was at this time the players asked Eagleson to help them. Eagleson organized every team despite formidable opposition. In 1967, in Montreal with myself, as the first president, we told the owners that the players in the NHL had formed an association and that Mr. Eagleson would be representing them in any further meetings with the owners. The owners accepted this and the NHL Player's Association was formed with Eagleson as their Director and myself as President. Eagleson, over the years did more for the hockey players than any other individual and players of today owe Mr. Eagleson a great deal, because without, Eagleson there would not have been an association .

In 1972, I retired as a player and became coach of the Los Angeles Kings. I was now on the other side of the table from Eagleson. Eagleson always represented his players first and never let our friendship effect his decisions. Once I wanted a player called David Hutchinson and made an offer for this player. Eagleson sent the player to Toronto because they offered Hutchinson more money.

Continued.........

CHICAGO BLACKHAWK HOCKEY TEAM, INC.
1901 West Madison Street, Chicago, IL 60612-2459 phone (312) 455-7000
Season Tickets: 680 North Lake Shore Drive, 19th Floor, Chicago, IL 60611-3084 phone (312) 943-7000 fax (312) 787-5553

Appendix B
Pulford Letter

December 5, 1997   Page 2

In 1977, I moved to Chicago and become the General Manager of the Chicago Blackhawks, a position I held until this July, 1997. During these years I served on the owner's committee in Collective Bargaining and with the owner's on the International Committee. During these years Al Eagleson was a tough negotiator, but always fair and honest who was able to get the benefits for the players and still keep the game of hockey first.

During all these years Al Eagleson never gave me one favor because of our friendship. He once said, "Business is business and friendship is friendship and the two cannot be mixed."

There has been a lot written about a player called Jim Harrison while he was with the Blackhawks. Harrison claims Eagleson did not look after him nothing could be farther from the truth. Jim Harrison was sent to the minor leagues by me and did not report saying he had a bad back. However, he had played the night before and never said anything to the trainers. When Harrison would not report I suspended him and stopped paying his salary. Al Eagleson called for a hearing in front of the President of the NHL. Al Eagleson discovered that I had suspended Harrison from Chicago and that Harrison should have been suspended by the minor league team, therefore the suspension was illegal and the Blackhawks had to pay Harrison.

In conclusion, Al Eagleson has been my friend for over forty years. Al Eagleson has been my advisor and family lawyer for over forty years. Al Eagleson represented me as a player in the NHL for 16 years. I was the first President of the NHL Player's Association and worked with Eagleson there for five years. I have been a General Manager for twenty years in the NHL and have sat across the table from Eagleson on many labor negotiations.

I think I am a good judge of people. Al Eagleson is a loyal friend. His integrity is unquestionable. He is a person that is always ready to help you without hesitation. Al Eagleson is a person who has done a tremendous amount of good in his lifetime, and I would request that you give him every favorable consideration. It is easy to pick any man's life apart. I would suggest that this be balanced by a review of all the good things he has done.

Yours truly,

Robert J. Pulford
Senior Vice-President

INDEX